How to Raise
Boys' Achievement

How to Raise Boys' Achievement

Colin Noble,
Jerry Brown and
Jane Murphy

David Fulton Publishers
London

David Fulton Publishers Ltd
The Chiswick Centre, 414 Chiswick High Road, London W4 5TF
www.fultonpublishers.co.uk

First published in Great Britain in 2001 by David Fulton Publishers

Note: The rights of Colin Noble, Jerry Brown and Jane Murphy to be identified
as the authors of this work have been asserted by them in accordance with the
Copyright, Designs and Patents Act 1988.

David Fulton Publishers is a division of Granada Learning Limited, part of
Granada plc.

British Library Cataloguing in Publication Data
A catalogue record for this book is available from the British Library.

ISBN 1-85346-825-8

Typeset by FiSH Books, London
Printed and bound in Great Britain

Contents

To Chris, Sarah, Stephen, Daniel and Nicola

Introduction

I wish there were no age between 10 and 23, because young men get wenches with child, upset the ancientry, stealing and fighting.

(William Shakespeare, *The Winter's Tale*)

The issue

Better build schoolrooms for 'the boy'
Than cells and gibbets for 'the man'.

(Eliza Cook, 'A Song for Ragged Schools', 1853)

It has been recognised since the mid 1990s that some boys are not achieving as well as they could do at school. The national, and international, concern that has been expressed is based partially on the narrow need of schools to improve their standards and 'meet their targets', but also more altruistically on a perception that significant numbers of young men are being let down in some way. Others have realised that it is in the enlightened self-interest of society to avoid spawning large numbers of 16–24-year-old males who have under-achieved, are under-skilled, under-employable but also under pressure to make their mark. Every under-achieving boy (and girl) is a small tragedy for the individual; but a cohort of under-achieving men will be a huge problem for any society. It is verging on a truism to point out distressed girls tend to vent their frustrations on themselves; distressed men tend to find other victims.

At conferences, courses and schools all over the country some will become indignant about this concern. Why is there all this fuss about boys when girls were allowed to under-achieve for decades? Why should we be bothered when it seems to most observers that boys are the authors of their own misfortune? The aggression, arrogance and anti-work culture of some boys, the argument goes, do not make them worthy recipients of any strategy, let alone one which unfairly takes the focus of teaching away from girls. The answer is twofold: firstly it is in all our interests to minimise the number of under-achieving boys and girls; and secondly that in finding ways to address effectively boys' under-achievement there is a great opportunity for establishing and embedding good educational practice for all pupils.

1

This book, and how to use it

This book offers a logical way to understand the issues and to take effective action in any school in any phase of schooling. Chapter 1 examines the messages about boys' achievement that can be gleaned from data, and suggests strategies for schools to use to monitor and analyse their own situation. Chapter 2 examines the reasons why boys under-achieve and includes a toolkit to use with school staff for discussing the particular situation of boys. Chapter 3 suggests a framework for planning effective strategies, and Chapters 4 and 6 discuss a menu of whole-school and classroom strategies from which to choose. Chapter 5 is entirely devoted to the sometimes difficult issue of engaging parents in helping to raise boys' achievement.

Embedding good school and classroom practice for race and social class

Other authors (Noble and Bradford 2000) have posed the question: do boys provide a more sensitive barometer of good quality teaching and learning than girls? In other words, does their focus, effort, performance and behaviour vary quite predictably with the quality of their learning experience, whereas girls are more likely to accept and absorb poor quality teaching? Discussions with teaching colleagues from all over the country and from many different types of schools suggest this is the case. It leaves us with a tantalising possibility. If getting it right for boys is basically good practice, then we should be able to benefit all learners from so called 'boys' achievement strategies'.

We have found it impossible to ignore the fact that the relative under-achievement of some boys is often inextricably interwoven with issues of ethnicity and socio-economic class. We have attempted to examine and cross-refer some of these issues throughout the book, partially because they are so compelling; but also – and far more significantly – we believe that if schools succeed in getting it right for boys they invariably get it right for pupils from under-achieving socio-economic classes and under-achieving minority ethnic groups.

The question may legitimately be asked, why are we using boys' or gender achievement as the window to good practice? Why not ethnicity or class? The answer is pragmatic: everybody is very clear about their gender and it is usually one of the main ways they define themselves. Everybody is *engaged* with gender, has experienced its expectations and demands, and has some understanding of the issues around it. This cannot be said of class or ethnicity. Although more powerful in their influence on attainment than gender these two issues are – in varying degrees – confusing, vague, threatening, irrelevant or even taboo to large numbers of schools, teachers, parents and pupils. We are not suggesting for one minute that they should be ignored, but we want to explore a path to effectively address them through focusing on boys' and girls' achievement.

This book is intended to appeal to several groups of people within education. It is primarily a practical book offering strategies which can be discussed, used, amended, rejected, passed on and contribute to helping build professional reflection and better practice. Primary and secondary teachers, LEA and Learning Skills Councils' officers, Higher Education students and lecturers will all find insights into the problem of, and solutions to, raising boys' achievement. The strategies proposed are also designed to raise the confidence, quality of participation in learning and achievement of girls.

1 Using data

Differences in test scores between boys and girls

The task of LEAs in administering an 11+ exam that is fair to all candidates is further complicated by the fact, established by evidence from a number of sources, that the performance of girls is superior to that of boys in most if not all the tests commonly employed.

(Transfer at Eleven Plus: a summary of evidence provided by research.
Educational Research, NFER VI, 1958)

As the quote above suggests, differences between boys' and girls' performance in academic tests have been known about for many years. Not only is there a gap but it is also getting larger. Table 1.1 shows the O level/GCE/GCSE achievements of all pupils since 1974/75; girls have been more successful than boys since 1977/78. Standards have risen tremendously for both but whereas in 1974/75 the gap between girls' and boys' attainment was only 0.8 per cent, by 1999/00 it had grown to 10.6 per cent.

Table 1.1 O Level/GCE/GCSE achievements of pupils in all schools in England 1974/75 to 2000/01

Percentage achieving 5 or more grades A*-C							
School leavers – any age				Pupils aged 15 at start of academic year			
Year	All	Boys	Girls	Year	All	Boys	Girls
1974/75	22.6	22.2	23.0	1988/89	32.8	29.8	35.8
1975/76	22.9	22.7	23.1	1989/90	34.5	30.8	38.4
1976/77	23.5	23.4	23.5	1990/91	36.8	33.3	40.3
1977/78	23.7	23.7	23.6	1991/92	38.3	34.1	42.7
1978/79	23.7	23.5	23.9	1992/93	41.2	36.8	45.8
1979/80	24.0	23.7	24.4	1993/94	43.3	39.1	47.8
1980/81	25.0	24.5	25.6	1994/95	43.5	39.0	48.1
1981/82	26.1	25.4	26.8	1995/96	44.5	39.9	49.4
1982/83	26.2	25.4	27.1	1996/97	45.1	40.5	50.0
1983/84	26.7	26.3	27.2	1997/98	46.3	41.3	51.5
1984/85	26.9	26.3	27.4	1999/00	49.2	44.0	54.6
1985/86	26.7	26.2	27.2				
1986/87	26.4	25.6	27.2				
1987/88	29.9	28.2	31.7				

Source: Statistics of Education: Public examinations GCSE/GNVQ and GCE/AGNVQ in England 2001

Such gender differences are an aspect of the majority of tests and examinations pupils in England and Wales sit today. Table 1.2 shows the difference in girls' and boys' performance in the key stage statutory tests, GCSE and A level in 2000.

Table 1.2 Pupils' Standards of Attainment Key Stages 1, 2, 3 and GCSE and GCE: Year 2001

			All (%)	Boys (%)	Girls (%)	Difference (%)
Key Stage 1 (Test/Task)	Level 2+	Reading	84.4	80.7	88.2	−7.5
		Writing	86.1	82.2	90.2	−8.0
		Mathematics	91.2	90.3	92.1	−1.8
	Level 3+	Reading	29.8	25.2	32.5	−7.3
		Writing	9.4	6.7	12.1	−5.4
		Mathematics	27.6	30.1	25.0	+5.1
Key Stage 2 (Test/Task)	Level 4+	English	75.1	70.2	80.2	−10.0
		Mathematics	70.7	71.3	70.1	+1.2
		Science	87.8	87.7	88.0	−0.3
	Level 5+	English	28.0	22.0	34.1	−12.1
		Mathematics	24.6	26.4	22.8	+3.6
		Science	33.7	34.3	33.1	−1.2
Key Stage 3 (Test/Task)	Level 5+	English	65.1	57.3	73.2	−15.9
		Mathematics	67.1	66.5	67.7	−1.2
		Science	66.6	67.1	66.0	+1.1
	Level 6+	English	32.0	25.4	38.8	−13.4
		Mathematics	42.9	42.6	43.1	+0.5
		Science	34.1	34.8	33.2	+1.6
GCSE		5+ A*–C	48.8	43.6	54.1	−10.5
		1+ A*–G	96.0	95.5	96.5	−1.0
		APS	39.1	36.6	41.5	−5.2
A Levels/ Advanced GNVQ results (Year 2000)	All subjects	Grades A–C	28.9	33.3	−4.4	
		Grades A–E	66.8	72.2	−5.4	

Source: Statistical Profile for Education in Schools, OFSTED, January 2002

The table shows that girls outperform boys in the vast majority of tests and examinations. The variation in the size of the gap stands out just as starkly if one looks at the differences in boys' and girls' performance across the most popular GCSE subjects (Table 1.3) with more girls than boys attaining A–C grades in 13 out of the 14 subjects, the difference being the greatest in the Arts and Social Sciences and the smallest in the sciences.

Table 1.3 Pupils' Standards of Attainment at GCSE 2001 in the subjects of the National Curriculum

Subject	% A*-C			
	All	Boys	Girls	Difference
English	58.6	50.7	66.4	−15.7
Mathematics	50.8	50.2	51.4	−1.2
Science (Dual Award)	57.6	50.3	52.9	−2.6
Physics	89.8	90.4	88.9	+1.5
Chemistry	89.9	89.2	90.8	−1.6
Biology	89.8	89.5	90.1	−0.6
History	61.3	58.4	64.1	−5.7
Geography	59.5	56.6	63.2	−6.6
Music	69.7	64.8	73.5	−8.7
PE	53.3	52.0	55.5	−3.5
CDT	51.6	43.6	59.9	−16.3
French	57.4	43.7	58.5	−14.8
German	56.0	49.2	62.3	−13.1
Art	65.4	53.9	74.7	−20.8

Source: Statistics of Education: Public examinations GCSE/GNVQ and GCE/AGNVQ in England 2000/01

Gender is not the only variable that has an impact on achievement. Class, race, ability and age also impact as well.

The impact of class on pupil attainment

Pupils from disadvantaged socio-economic backgrounds do not do as well in the statutory tasks and tests as pupils from more advantaged backgrounds. Table 1.4 shows the median Key Stage 2 test scores of schools with different proportions of pupils entitled to free school meals (a proxy measure of social deprivation) in 2000.

Table 1.4 Median scores of Key Stage 2, schools grouped according to DfEE Autumn Package Bands: Year 2002 results

Free School Meal Band	Median Score English (% 4+)	Median Score Mathematics (% 4+)	Median Score Science (% 4+)
8%	86	84	94
8–20%	77	76	90
20–35%	68	67	85
35–50%	60	61	79
50%	55	60	72

Source: Autumn Package of Pupil Performance Information, DfEE, 2002

Schools with the highest proportion of pupils entitled to free school meals do less well in all the tests than schools with smaller proportions. Only 56 per cent of pupils in schools with 50 per cent or more pupils eligible for free school meals attained Level 4+ in English while 87 per cent attained Level 4+ in schools which had 8 per cent or fewer pupils eligible for free school meals.

The impact of race on pupil attainment

Pupils' results also vary according to their ethnic background, and girls outperform the boys of the same ethnic group. For example, Table 1.5 ranks pupils' performance in the tests and GCSE by both ethnic background and gender. Indian girls and UK, Irish, European girls are generally high attainers and Pakistani and Afro-Caribbean girls are generally low attainers but in all cases they all perform better than boys of the same ethnic group.

Table 1.5 Average per cent score 2000 across all key stage and GCSE by gender and ethnicity

Average per cent score 2000 across all key stage subjects/GCSE 5+A*-C				
Rank	KS1	KS2	KS3	GCSE
1	Girls (I)	Girls (O)	Girls (O)	Girls (O)
2	Girls (P)	Girls (I)	Girls (UKIE)	Girls (UKIE)
3	Boys (O)	Boys (I)	Girls (I)	Girls (I)
4	Girls (AC)	Girls (UKIE)	Boys (I)	Boys (UKIE)
5	Girls (UKIE)	Boys (AC)	Boys (UKIE)	Girls (P)
6	Boys (I)	Boys (UKIE)	Girls (P)	Boys (I)
7	Boys (UKIE)	Girls (AC)	Boys (O)	Boys (P)
8	Boys (AC)	Boys (O)	Boys (AC)	Girls (AC)
9	Girls (O)	Boys (P)	Boys (P)	Boys (O)
10	Boys (P)	Girls (P)	Girls (AC)	Boys (AC)

(I) – Indian, (P) – Pakistani, (AC) – African Caribbean, (UKIE) – UK, Irish, European, (O) – Other

Source: *Authors' analysis*

The impact of age on pupil attainment

Pupils' age also has a significant impact on their subsequent levels of attainment. Table 1.6 shows that pupils who are born in the first term of an academic year generally perform better in the Key Stage 1 and 2 tests than pupils who are born in the Spring and Summer terms. For instance, girls with birthdays in September, October, November or December attained 28 average points across the Key Stage 2 tests while girls with birthdays in May, June, July and August only attained 26.6 points.

Table 1.6 Pupils' Standards of Attainment across a Local Education Authority Key Stages 1 and 2 – differentiated by term of birth

		Average Point Score			
		Autumn Term (A)	Spring Term	Summer Term (S)	Difference (A–S)
	Girl	28.0	27.0	26.6	1.4
KS2	Boy	27.3	26.6	26.4	0.9
	Difference	0.7	0.4	0.2	
	Girl	15.7	14.6	13.9	1.8
KS1	Boy	14.7	13.9	13.5	1.2
	Difference	1.0	0.7	0.4	

Source: *Authors' analysis*

Table 1.6 also shows that no matter which term a child is born in, girls do better than boys born in that same term. The gap in the differences is not, however, constant across the terms, the difference being greatest between boys and girls born in the Autumn term, and the least for boys and girls born in the Summer term. Differences in pupil attainment attributable to age are not just a feature of primary school assessments but continue to GCSE.

Table 1.7 Pupils' Standards of Attainment across a Local Education Authority GCSE 2000 – differentiated by term of birth

	GCSE (% 5+A*-Cs)			
	Autumn Term (A)	Spring Term	Summer Term (S)	Difference (A–S)
Girl	55	50	46	9
Boy	41	40	38	3
Difference	14	10	8	

Source: *Authors' analysis*

Table 1.7 shows the differences in pupil attainment at GCSE by age and gender. Yet again, the highest attainers are girls who were born in the Autumn term and the lowest boys born in the Summer term. Of great concern is the fact that boys who are born in the Autumn term do not perform even as well as the lowest attaining girls born in the Summer term. Another interesting observation is the fact that the difference in performance of girls is greater than that of boys. Nine per cent more Autumn born girls attain five or more A*-C grades than Summer born girls; for boys, the gap is only 3 per cent.

The impact of ability on pupil attainment

There is some evidence to suggest that a pupil's general ability may also impact with gender on the pupil's subsequent level of attainment. Table 1.8 shows differences in pupils' levels of attainment at GCSE by gender and by type of school attended, selective schools having the smallest difference of 1.6 per cent and modern schools the greatest of 12.1 per cent.

Table 1.8 GCSE achievements 1998/99

School type	% 5+A*-C GCSE
Comprehensive schools	
All	46.5
Boys	41.1
Girls	52.0
Selective schools	
All	96.7
Boys	95.9
Girls	97.5
Modern schools	
All	34.0
Boys	27.9
Girls	40.0

Source: *Statistics of Education: Public examinations GCSE/GNVQ and GCE/AGNVQ in England 1999*

It could be argued that this difference between types of schools might be a consequence of pupils' levels of innate ability: the pupils with the highest innate ability – those chosen to go to selective schools – have the smallest differences between girls' and boys' performance and the pupils with the lowest innate ability – those going to modern schools – having the greatest differences. This, however, does not appear to be a viable argument. Table 1.9 shows pupils' performance at GCSE grouped not only by gender but by a measure of prior attainment – their Key Stage 3 average points score.

Looking at Table 1.9, the difference between girls' and boys' attainment hardly differs across the ability spectrum, being 0.3 for those pupils who have 25 or fewer average points at Key Stage 3, and 0.4 for those who attained 38 or more points.

What this indicates to the practitioner is that if one wants to minimise the gap between girls' and boys' levels of attainment, one shouldn't have modern schools.

All this data suggests that if you wished to predict at birth which child would have the best chance of being successful in the English educational system you would be wise to choose an Indian girl who was born in September or October, and who was not eligible for free school meals.

Table 1.9 GCSE average points score grouped by gender and prior attainment

KS2	GCSE average points		
	Boys	Girls	Difference
Prior attainment (average points score)			
<= 25	2.0	2.3	0.3
26 <= – <= 30	3.0	3.3	0.3
31 <= – <= 33	3.8	4.1	0.3
34 <= – <= 37	4.6	5.1	0.5
=> 38	5.8	6.2	0.4

Source: *Authors' analysis*

Using data to tackle underperformance

Given that the test and examination data does show that there is a gap between boys' and girls' performance, why should we be bothered about it? Perhaps the gap is natural. Using the data, it could be argued that girls are naturally higher attainers than boys. Would perhaps our male dominated society be so concerned about the differences in results if the gap were the other way about?

There is the possibility that, no matter what teachers and schools do, the gap cannot be closed. What is of importance, perhaps, is not the fact that there is a gap but the variation of the size of the gap between schools.

Table 1.10 shows the GCSE results of 22 high schools in a local authority in 2000. The gap between girls and boys in respect to the proportion of each attaining A*-C grades varies in English from 30 per cent to 3 per cent.

Interpreting such data is difficult. Firstly, what does it tell us about each school's effectiveness? Are schools U and V, where the gap between boys and girls is narrowest, the most effective schools in tackling boys' under-attainment in English? Or, could it be argued that girls are under-performing, that they should be doing better and that, on average, they should be doing better than boys by at least the national difference. Secondly, what impact do such figures have on teachers' expectations and on the process of target setting? Should teachers expect the same levels of attainment from boys as they do from girls? Or, in English, should they expect 17 per cent (the national average) more girls to attain A*-C grades than boys and be satisfied if they do? If teachers are setting targets for pupils, should they set the same targets for girls and boys, or higher targets for boys than for girls? To some extent whatever they do, they are opening themselves to criticism.

The pragmatic answer to these issues is, perhaps, for teachers to accept that there is a difference in performance between boys and girls, that they should be aware of this and, according to their results, they should be asking whether or not one of the groups is under-achieving.

Table 1.10 Boy/Girl difference

A*-C 2000 results (%) English GCSE across 22 high schools			
English			
School	Boys	Girls	Difference
A	53	84	−31
B	25	54	−29
C	60	87	−27
D	31	57	−26
E	25	51	−26
F	24	49	−25
G	21	46	−25
H	47	69	−22
I	20	40	−20
J	43	61	−18
K	43	61	−18
L	52	68	−16
M	32	47	−15
N	35	49	−14
O	32	46	−14
P	66	79	−13
Q	48	58	−10
R	31	37	−6
S	66	71	−5
T	52	55	−3
U	97	100	−3
V	50	52	−2

Source: *Authors' analysis*

Using data to promote attainment

Schools are now data rich environments. They have moved from a position 15 years ago when the majority of pupils sat no formal tests or examinations until they were 15 to one where children are formally assessed in the Foundation Stage at 7, 11, 14 and GCSE. In addition to these assessments, teachers are encouraged to administer non-statutory assessments to their pupils at periodic intervals. This pupil level data along with national comparative data, provides teachers with the necessary tools to identify pupil under-achievement, set targets, monitor progress and evaluate performance.

Identifying pupil under-achievement

The QCA's Autumn Packs provide teachers with analyses of statutory end of key stage assessments and GCSE results in the form of value added and chances graphs. Teachers are encouraged to plot their own pupils' results onto these graphs. By doing so, they are able to identify groups of pupils who may be under-achieving and evaluate the overall effectiveness of their teaching. By ensuring that both boys' and girls' performance is identified in such analyses, it is possible to see whether one or both groups or a subset of either group is under-performing.

Setting targets

Setting targets for pupils is an incredibly powerful tool for raising attainment. The process of target setting itself is deceptively simple. Teachers are provided with historical pupil achievement data which in the QCA's Autumn Pack shows, for instance, the relationship between Key Stage 3 average points scores and their subsequent GCSE results. Provided that a teacher knows subsequent pupils' Key Stage 3 average points scores, they can predict with some degree of reliability the pupils' results at GCSE. This prediction with an added degree of challenge becomes the pupil's target.

The quest to raise boys' attainment, however, introduces an ethical dimension into the process of target setting. Raising attainment is a relative concept. Against what is the change in attainment to be measured? If it is just an issue of trying to raise all pupils' attainment by ten per cent, for example in GCSE English, then there is no ethical problem because presumably, both boys' and girls' attainment will rise by this amount. But what are the equal opportunities implications of focusing on raising boys' attainment by five per cent in order to close the gap between boys' and girls' attainment at GCSE from 17 per cent to 12 per cent? In order to effect this, more time and resources will have to be focused specifically on boys. Teachers and schools will have to develop boy friendly teaching and learning strategies. What will happen to girls' levels of attainment? Are we happy if they remain static while boys' standards rise? The answer to this last question is, of course, 'No'.

In order to ensure that target setting does not result in girls being disadvantaged, it is important that schools and teachers have clear goals and expectations of what they are hoping to achieve when they begin the process. An analysis of a school's English GCSE results 2000 might show that 24 per cent of girls attained A*-C grades in English compared to only 3 per cent of boys – a gap of 21 per cent and 4 per cent greater than the national gap. It would be valid for the school to set itself two targets: firstly, to narrow the gap between girls' and boys' attainment to that of the national average; and secondly, to raise the attainment of all pupils by an extra ten per cent. If both these targets were successfully achieved, in 2003 boys' attainment in English would have risen by 14 per cent.

One way schools and teachers can monitor their target setting expectations is to set up a spreadsheet similar to Spreadsheet 1.1.

School:	%
Aggregate target in English	
Aggregate target in Maths	

	%
Indicative target English	
Indicative target Maths	

	%
Agreed LEA target English	
Agreed LEA target Maths	

Ethnic group	No. in cohort			No. English L4+			No. Maths L4+			% English L4+			% Maths L4+		
Gender	M	F	All	M	F	All	M	F	All	M	F	All	M	F	All
White/UK/Irish W1															
White European W2															
Black African B1															
Black Caribbean B2															
Black Other B3															
Indian A1															
Pakistani A2															
Bangladeshi A3															
Mixed race – Asian M1															
Mixed race – African/Caribbean M2															
Mixed race – European M3															
Any other minority ethnic group															
Total															

Spreadsheet 1.1

To set the target, teachers need to first compile a pupil list which should give a measure of their prior attainment, their ethnic background and their gender. The teacher should then consider each pupil in turn, setting them an individual target based on their prior attainment, the teacher's knowledge of them and the expectation of their achieving a certain outcome in the future. When this has been done for each pupil, the teacher then needs to complete the spreadsheet. As can be seen in the completed example (Spreadsheet 1.2), this raises some interesting questions about teacher expectations. For instance, why does the teacher expect a smaller proportion of Pakistani pupils to achieve Level 4+ in English and mathematics than white pupils, and why, for all ethnic groups and the class overall, does the teacher expect boys to do less well than girls in both subjects?

Using a spreadsheet such as this one is not only a useful way of raising issues regarding teacher expectation, it is also an extremely useful way of analysing the final results of a class and shows up differences not only between girls and boys, but also between different ethnic groups, and girls and boys in different ethnic groups.

School: Any School	%
Aggregate target in English	63
Aggregate target in Maths	59

	%
Indicative target English	
Indicative target Maths	

	%
Agreed LEA target English	
Agreed LEA target Maths	

Ethnic group	No. in cohort			No. English L4+			No. Maths L4+			% English L4+			% Maths L4+		
Gender	M	F	All	M	F	All	M	F	All	M	F	All	M	F	All
White/UK/Irish W1	25	27	52	13	20	33	10	22	32	52	74	63	40	81	62
White European W2															
Black African B1															
Black Caribbean B2															
Black Other B3															
Indian A1															
Pakistani A2	17	13	30	8	11	19	7	9	16	47	85	63	41	69	53
Bangladeshi A3															
Mixed race – Asian M1															
Mixed race – African/Caribbean M2															
Mixed race – European M3															
Any other minority ethnic group															
Total	42	40	82	21	31	52	17	31	48	50	78	63	40	78	59

Spreadsheet 1.2 Completed spreadsheet allowing analysis of targets and teacher expectations by gender and ethnic background

Monitoring progress

Of course, it is no use just setting targets and then waiting until the end of the key stage to see whether or not pupils attain them. Once targets have been set, teachers have to monitor pupils' progress towards them. A very neat model which allows such monitoring to take place across Key Stage 2 is shown in Table 1.11.

Pupils are grouped according to their prior attainment at the end of Key Stage 1. A target can then be established for them, not only for the end of the key stage but also for the end of Years 7 and 8. For instance, a pupil who attained an average points score of 15 (Level 2b) at the end of Key Stage 1 could be judged to be an average pupil and should be expected to attain Level 4b (27) or 4a (29) at the end of Key Stage 2. Teachers could, therefore, expect the pupil, if he or she made consistent progress towards this outcome, to be attaining an average points score of 17 at the end of Year 3, 21 at the end of Year 4 and 25 at the end of Year 5. If the pupil's progress is less than this, then the teacher needs to intervene. Of course, pupils who have a higher prior

Table 1.11 School self evaluation of Standards of Attainment at Key Stages 1 and 2 by test and task and gender

	National (2000)		School (2000)	
	Boys better	Girls better	Boys better	Girls better
Key Stage 1 (% 2+)				
Reading		+9		+13
Writing		+9		+9
Spelling	Same	Same		+1
Mathematics		+2		+2
Key Stage 2 (% 4+)				
English		+9		+9
Mathematics	+1		+2	
Science		+1	Same	Same

attainment score at the beginning of Year 3 will have a higher target set for them for the end of Year 6 and will, therefore, be expected to make more progress over the intervening years. Pupils with lower prior attainment scores may, perhaps, be expected to do less well, make less progress and, at the end of Year 6, attain a lower level.

The usefulness of this as a model for supporting target setting and monitoring pupil progress is that it takes no account of gender. It looks at a pupil's potential based on his or her prior attainment. Any pupils who attained an average points score of 15 at the end of Key Stage 1 should, reasonably, be expected to attain an average points score of 27 at the end of Key Stage 2. The teacher's expectations are determined by prior attainment, not a pupil's gender or ethnic origin.

Schools should also monitor their own results in terms of gender, completing a table such as the one in Table 1.12. In this completed example, the gender differences are in line with national differences in respect to all test and task results at Key Stages 1 and 2, apart from in reading at Key Stage 1. Again, such monitoring allows the school to focus its attention on designing strategies to raise boys' attainment in a specific area of the curriculum. Such a targeted approach is much more likely to be effective than one which is more open-ended and aimed at raising boys' attainment across the curriculum.

Table 1.12 Target Indicator Table Key Stage 2: English, mathematics and science

	Key Stage 1 Result	End of Year 3 Target	End of Year 4 Target	End of Year 5 Target	Key Stage 2 Target	Other Indicators Age Standardised Scores
Special Needs	W	Targets for Special Needs pupils will be set by a different process				−130
Well below average	1(9)	2c (13)	2b (15)	3c (19)	3b (21)	70–85
Below average	2c (13)	2b (15)	3c (19)	3a (23)	3/4 (4 target) (25)	86–93
Average	2b (15)	2a (17)	3b (21)	4c (25)	4b (27)	94–108
Above average	2a (17)	3c (19)	3a (23)	4b (27)	4/5 (5 target) (31)	109–115
Well above average	3b (21)	3a (23)	4b (27)	5c (31)	5a (35)	116–130
Special Needs, Gifted children	4+ (27+)	Targets for gifted children will be set by a different process				130+

Source: Adapted from a model developed by Cogent Computer Software Ltd and published in the *Times Educational Supplement's Magic Mark Book* 2000

2 Why do boys under-achieve?

In Chapter 1 you have had the opportunity to analyse the national data and have been encouraged to examine the situation in your own school. The purpose of this chapter is to explore the possible reasons *why* some boys are under-achieving. In some ways this could be seen as an interesting but ultimately fruitless debate: we have to deal with the situation we find, and should not waste time in debating its genesis. If, however, we do not understand the reasons why some boys are as they are we may come up with some inappropriate strategies.

The reasons why boys under-achieve

Probably the most debatable aspect of the generally controversial issue of boys' achievement is that of the cause of the problem. It is rich territory for the nature versus nurture debaters. Although the arguments normally engender more heat than light it is a valuable one to be had if you are interested in bringing about change. It *does* capture interest and reflection and forces the different sides to focus on the nature of learning, gender characteristics and pupils as individuals. The debate itself can be a catalyst for change.

In some ways it does not matter what the causes of boys' under-achievement may be. Teachers and the education establishment in general have to work with the situation before them, and its source – obscure, complex and controversial – may be interesting but hardly useful. It is the practical strategies which teachers are most concerned with. Unless, however, we have some understanding of the background causes we may be adopting plans and policies which are wholly inappropriate to the problem.

> Much of the response has to be site-specific and based on a thorough, sensitive collection and analysis of local data.
>
> (Epstein *et al.*, p. 14)

Boys and the 'anti-swot' culture*

(Note that in some parts of the country this may be known as anti-bof, anti-keeno or anti-square culture.)*

Some teachers have argued with conviction that we are in danger of over-complicating a very simple fact: some boys don't work as hard as most girls. They tend to be lazier, less motivated, less organised, poorer presenters and less eager to please. In some schools, they positively promote an anti-swot culture that both justifies their own behaviour and challenges the rights of other boys, and occasionally girls, to try hard. This argument is difficult to refute but far too reductionist. It leaves two fundamental questions unanswered: why is this culture so prevalent when many boys *do* want to work hard and succeed in doing so; and secondly, where has this culture come from? The simple diagnosis tends to promote a simple prescription – let's change the culture of boys. This is laudable, but without knowing more about its genesis it is impossible to understand the mechanisms and direction of change. We are suggesting that there are six main reasons why boys are presently achieving less than girls at school. Not everybody will agree with them or give them the titles we have, but it will help the discussion in your workplace.

Six possible reasons why boys presently achieve less than girls

1. Genetic

This is the sort of thing which will leave female colleagues cheering and alienate the males. Are women really more intelligent than men? Has their natural superiority been oppressed by centuries of male domination? Is their true potential only showing itself now as we enter an age of generally increasing equality? We have no idea! There is a certain amount of evidence that women may have an intuitive or genetic disposition to be better communicators than men. Research, mainly in the United States, suggests that new born babies show clear gender differences in their ability to understand and discriminate between sounds. Surrey LEA found three-year-old boys and girls have marked differences in linguistic abilities; and the Key Stage 1 SATs show a gender gap at seven which is rarely shortened over the next nine years of schooling.

Darwinists have argued that the reason for this gap, for the large phone bills which are the rites of passage for teenage girls, and for the GCSE differences go back to the roles which women and men have played for thousands of years. Women have always been the nurturers, the talkers, the makers of homes and occupiers of kitchens where conversation is not only possible but necessary. Men on the other hand have tended to take on more isolated roles, whether it be hunter-gatherers, tillers or herdsmen. It is only in fairly recent times in the span of human history that these roles have changed. It will be some time yet before evolution catches up with the needs of the modern male.

The most significant development in this field in recent years has been the greater knowledge of how the brain works, gender differences in its physiology and the possible implications for teaching and learning. The finding that women tend to make greater use of both hemispheres, and the suggestion that the cortex connecting them is more robust and more frequently used in the female head (Shaw and Hawes 1998) is fascinating and possibly valuable information. We do feel, however, that a large note of caution is necessary. Although there is *greater* knowledge, scientists are a long way from really understanding the full picture. Secondly, the results of brain gender research have tended to excite some of its proponents into proposing quick-fix, classroom based solutions. These tend to ignore the critical contribution of the whole-school approach and – far more importantly – forget that many girls and boys do not fit in to the biologically-determined stereotypes ascribed to them. We do not dismiss the brain research, and discuss it in Chapter 6, but it should be viewed as yet another reason for ensuring a variety of teaching and learning styles are employed for both genders.

2. Changes in society

> And the men shall come singing from the fields, for they have provided for their own.
>
> (Old English proverb (apparently) quoted in
Heinz tomato soup television advertisement)

Society has changed so quickly over the last three decades that it is sometimes difficult for us to know exactly how things are different from a generation ago. Most adults, even those in regular contact with young people, often tend to judge present youthful experiences from a 20- or 30-year-old perspective. The environment in which children and young people grow up has changed radically, and looks as if it will continue to do so.

> The social upheavals of the last 25 years – feminist challenges, unemployment, the collapse of the male bread winner and the traditional father as head of the household, the emergence of HIV/AIDS and de-industrialisation – have unsettled the traditional models of dominant, white, heterosexual masculinities.
>
> (David Jackson, in Epstein *et al.*, p. 79)

We have no intention of examining or listing all these changes, but there are some which have had a radical impact upon the life chances of males and affected the way many of them think about themselves.

Possibly the most important change has been in the field of employment. For many boys who were of below average academic ability in the 1960s there was little difficulty in finding a job, although this may have varied with the economic cycle. Labouring, factory work, the coalmines, shipyards and steel mills, semi-skilled jobs on the railway were all available, sometimes through apprenticeship schemes, and they paid wages which enabled the worker to make his way and raise a family. Moreover, there were millions of people doing this. It was an expectation, a normality, and the workers from whom the young apprentices learned were other men who often had a respect derived from their experience and skill. There were few problems in identifying a path to follow. It may not have been a particularly exciting or visionary expectation by today's standards – but it was valued by all those around. This culture predates the revolution of expectation, when the idea that a favourite hobby could be listed as 'shopping' would be incomprehensible. Having a great deal of disposable income and non-essential goods in the shops to purchase, had not yet reached the vast majority of working people.

> The factory of the future will have two employees: a man and a dog. The man is there to feed the dog, and the dog is there to ensure the man doesn't meddle with the machinery.
>
> (Anonymous – urban myth, often quoted to capture technological changes)

The shopping, advertising and commercialisation revolutions of the 1970s and 1980s have changed all of this. The growth of the importance of image and style has coincided with the demise of millions of engineering, technical, colliery, shipyard and steel jobs. They, and the communities they supported, were bastions of male values and male hegemony. They have largely disappeared and in some parts of the country, for example South Yorkshire, one can still feel a sense of mourning because they have not been adequately replaced. A film like 'Brassed Off' effectively captured the beginning of that process while 'The Full Monty', underneath the humour and surrealism, says an awful lot about the breakdown of families, the need to be respected and the importance of male role models for boys. Both films were set in South Yorkshire and both depict a society left behind by technological changes.

What has replaced them are millions of new jobs in the service sector. Insurance, commerce, finance, tourism, clerical and other office based jobs do not need the sort of strength and skills men once used in the old industries. Instead, good communication skills and, often, good keyboard skills are demanded. They are often seen as 'women's jobs', and as most of the staff working in them are women, one can see why. Not only do they demand the sort of skills women have, these same skills are ones which men tend to lack. The old certainties and expectations have disappeared with the jobs, and this has had a dramatic effect upon boys and young men. The under-achieving seven year old is unlikely to blame technological change for his reluctance to try harder but, if pressed gently, he may say that the only people he knows who work hard are women. The girls in his class seem to work, his Mum, aunts and sister work but the males in his life resemble resting actors. There are some parts of the UK where for some time the women have been the only breadwinners in the family and the men have come to accept long-term unemployment as a way of life. The sons of these men, who may have never worked, have sometimes adopted a culture which is hard to challenge. This could be viewed as a rational adaptation to the real life-chances they have (Kress 1998). What alternative model is offered by the many critics of boys?

If girls are defined by their work ethic, how do boys define themselves?

In the absence of anything else, it may be that boys see that to be a boy means that you don't work. As he gets older this view is confirmed by the popular image of success. The TV advertisements, many films of modern life, men's magazines portray successful men as having fast cars, attractive women, designer clothes and exciting holidays. Alternatively, and this is more often the case since the turn of the century, they are portrayed as stupid but cheerful losers. They are seldom portrayed working, (although interestingly women are), and there seems therefore to be a causal connection between success and *not* working. The young man cannot quite rationalise this, but he buys into the image of success without quite knowing how it is achieved. Maybe it is achieved by being cool, by not trying too hard. In this context it is not surprising that some boys have developed the idea of effortless achievement. Schools would be ill-advised to use footballers as role models, unless they are prepared to talk about the value of their academic qualifications and the possibilities they open up. The age of working smart, not hard, has contributed to the anti-work culture. It is little wonder that the men are no longer singing as they come home from the fields.

3. Changes in families

> My mother cries in the middle of the night, too. She says she's worn out nursing and feeding and changing and four boys is too much for her. She wishes she had one little girl all for herself. She'd give anything for a girl.
>
> (*Angela's Ashes*, Frank McCourt, p. 14)

Just how much involvement fathers have with their children, and particularly their sons, varies enormously between families. An increasing number of families are cash-rich and time-poor. For many children this can mean they have never been so materially wealthy, but also that they have not received the emotional investment enjoyed by their parents when young. Surveys suggest (*The Observer*, 25 February 2001) that the 'new hooligans' are as likely to come from affluent backgrounds as deprived.

From being a country that luxuriated (admittedly at a cost) in working the shortest hours in Europe, the average UK worker now puts in the most hours in western Europe. Some fathers see their sons only at weekends, because of work reasons. Additionally, there are now 1,250,000 single parent families in the United Kingdom, and in the vast majority of cases they are headed by women. There are large numbers of boys who do not have significant adult males in their lives, and who may not see any male teachers at primary school. This is not just a case of a lack of a role model, which is important enough. Biddulph (1997) suggests that boys need a father figure when between 5 and 12 years old, after which an older male mentor becomes very important. If a child does not have any form of meaningful relationship with a male adult before the age of eleven, and sometimes after that, what does that child think about men? If the child is a boy, what does he think he will be growing up to be? He may not actually verbalise the feminist question 'What are men for?' because other forms of information fill the vacuum. Popular culture has a fairly lurid or glamorous view of men which has little connection with real

Table 2.1 Men, boys and responsibility

This table shows how the average age for boys and young men to take responsibility has changed since 1958		
	1958	**1998**
Leaving school	15/16	18
Leaving home	18	24
Marrying/living with	20	27
Becoming fathers	21	28
Source: *Working With Men*, conference in Lewisham, June 2000		

lives, but in the absence of anything more immediate boys have images and information which do not suggest that being a man is about working hard. (See Table 2.1.)

Surveys reveal that men are much less involved with the supervision of homework than women, tend to attend fewer parents' evenings and hear their children read less than mothers. Just to compound the crime, fathers are less demanding of their sons than their daughters. Girls are expected to be well-behaved, well presented, neat, organised, be keener readers, clean and conventional. Boys tend to be expected to be less mature, less responsible, more rebellious, dirtier, sportier, spottier, comparatively irresponsible, and with lower concentration spans. These expectations are often fulfilled. Many parents feel that there is no need to worry about their sons' learning until they get to secondary school, by which time it is often too late.

4. Curriculum reasons

The curriculum has changed. This should be no surprise. Following the second National Curriculum of 1995, its 'paring back' in 1998 and its full scale rewrite in 2000 teachers are tired of change. One of the reasons they could be disillusioned with permanent curriculum revolution has not often been voiced. The new curriculum tends to be more hostile to boys and this has had an effect upon their attitude, behaviour, effort and achievement.

In Key Stage 2, the curriculum is still overcrowded and teachers have generally responded in the obvious, possibly the only, way to this problem. Teaching has become more content and less process oriented. This penalises both genders, but particularly boys whose favoured learning styles are squeezed out by the exigencies of time and curriculum coverage.

In Key Stage 3, the curriculum is still crowded and the advent of league tables which reflect National Curriculum success has brought another change. Middle schools are being abolished as LEAs consider ways of making schools more co-terminus with the key stages and therefore more accountable for their results. In many authorities (e.g. Leeds and Bradford) the middle school system has gone. The arguments about middle schools are infinite, but there is some evidence that they were particularly good for boys. It is the Year 8 boy in secondary schools who is a prime candidate for first losing motivation, but in many middle schools he was in the top class and enjoyed high status (Bleach *et al.* 1998).

It is in Key Stage 4, where perhaps the most obvious boy-hostile curriculum changes have occurred. Many commentators suggest that GCSE courses are appropriate for only the top 60–70 per cent of the ability range within any subject. Yet nearly all are forced to follow the full National Curriculum. This is as true for girls as it is for boys, but boys respond differently. When they are bored, alienated or confused boys are less ready than girls to accept their lot, to knuckle down and work steadily towards their D, E or F grade. Conversely, girls' socialisation often depicts life as being a struggle and that hard work is to be expected.

The fairly recent ability of schools to disapply parts of the National Curriculum should help boys, but it is too early yet to judge this. Anecdotally, it seems that significantly more boys than girls are being 'disapplied'. The relief of dropping the dreaded modern foreign language, 'boring' history or disappointing technology ('disappointing' because there is more writing and less doing than anticipated) may help to motivate boys, but much depends on the quality of what replaces these subjects.

When still struggling with the National Curriculum boys are far more likely than girls to give up, disappear or draw attention by causing chaos. For those within the 60–70 per cent there is more bad news. The assessment methods used in GCSE are often partly based on project work or continual assessment. This suggests organised, long-term planning in a way which was less necessary in the days of end of course examinations. The results are plain to see in subjects like Design and Technology about which boys are often initially enthusiastic but under-perform compared to girls. It is interesting to see the results of schools which have adopted modular 'A' levels which give the sort of bite-sized, finite work to which boys relate far better.

In addition to this, there is some suggestion that parts of the curriculum itself are less favourable to boys. Do the set books in English favour stories which are predominantly concerned with relationships rather than action? The tasks set for English, often reflecting on feelings and emotions, seem easier to many girls who have more experience of it in their own lives. Is it not the case that ICT across the curriculum, something which boys would have generally found interesting, has in most instances been poorly implemented by schools? When it does exist it has often been little more than word processing, appealing to girls' strengths, rather than spreadsheets, databases and data-handling which are more often favoured by boys.

This is not an argument for changing the curriculum to favour boys, but rather to be aware of the potential effects upon boys – and girls – of changes to the curriculum and assessment methods, and to take account of this in school and classroom management.

To be fair to both boys and girls it is likely that a variety of assessment modes should be used so that all pupils have opportunities to produce their best performance.

(Arnot *et al.* 1998)

5. School management

School managers have had an awful lot to deal with in recent years. Aside from the massive changes to the curriculum, financial delegation, governors, league tables, parental pressure, OFSTED and a school population which mirrors the stresses in society, they also have had to manage a revolution in expectation of themselves. They are now monitors of the quality of teaching and learning and managers of change. It is not an easy job. Many also teach, which for some is a blessed relief from meetings, telephones, crises and reports. So it is with a sense of guilt that we write that school managers have also a large measure of responsibility for boys' under-achievement.

It is mainly by a neglect of what they could have done, rather than through what they have actually done, that managers should examine themselves. The lack, or lack of use in classrooms, of early data about pupil potential is still a large problem despite the huge amount of paperwork devoted to this area. The publishing of benchmark data in Key Stages 2, 3, and 4 might now help schools to focus on the potential of younger age groups, but school PANDAs (Performance and Assessments) still do not benchmark by gender difference. It is therefore still difficult to judge whether one school's gender–achievement gap is any better or worse than its neighbour's.

The acceptance of, or inability to tackle, the anti-swot culture is largely a management responsibility. It will be a recurring theme of this book that schools must be, and must portray themselves as, learning organisations. There should be no place for the anti-swot culture. Schools should treat it as they do racism; there should be no tolerance of it. It is an assault upon equal opportunities and results in misery and under-achievement. We shall be addressing this issue in Chapter 4.

Another recent phenomenon has been the re-introduction of setting and streaming in an increasing number of primary schools, and its spread to more subjects in secondary schools. It is evident that there is no perfect way of grouping pupils (Noble and Bradford 2000, Boaler 1996). All methods have advantages and disadvantages, but the most successful have two characteristics: (a) the staff using it believes in it; and (b) the inherent weaknesses in the system are recognised and addressed by intelligent and focused use of resources, time and training. Good teachers can compensate for bad grouping, but why make it hard for everyone? The rush towards setting in the past two years has often been at the expense of boys, as we explore later.

6. Classroom management

Most teachers in mixed schools are aware that there are two different genders in the classroom with them. They are also aware that these two genders can exhibit distinctly different sorts of behaviours; that they spend more time telling boys off; that boys tend to be less punctual, reliable, motivated and organised. What is less evident is teachers realising or accepting that there may be at least two different types of *learner* in the class. Seating policy, display and teaching and learning styles are addressed in later chapters but we want to make the point early in the book that teachers have an enormous amount of discretion in their classroom management which can either exacerbate or ameliorate the motivation and under-achievement of boys. There is no blueprint for success but there are techniques and strategies which have been tried in a number of schools and have been found successful (Shaw and Hawes 1998, Noble and Bradford 2000). Our experience of this work has witnessed the teacher reclaiming his or her confidence and skills as a creative professional who is prepared to try things out, sometimes fail, but more often succeed.

Boys from minority ethnic groups

This situation is made more complex when considering the relative under-achievement of boys from some minority ethnic groups. In Chapter 1, we found that Britain's minority ethnic groups varied considerably in their achievement. Much of this is attributable to class, e.g. Black and Asian boys from middle class backgrounds are far more likely to succeed than white boys from deprived backgrounds, but there are relatively few middle class Black and Asian families; and in some instances it is attributable to language. This does not, however, explain why, for example, boys of African descent achieve well in Key Stage 1 SATs but then, as a cohort, tend to fall behind their white peers. It appears that although socio-economic class is the most important factor in determining likely educational success, ethnicity and gender are still influential. The Black or mixed race boy, like all boys, at seven onwards begins to relate more with the wider world around him. What he sees may sometimes disappoint, worry or anger him.

> Black boys growing up in Britain today will often find they experience behaviour or attitudes, by *some* white people that they do not like. It may help to know why some people have such attitudes and behave in such nasty ways.
>
> The answer lies mainly in the history of enslavement and colonialism that lasted for hundreds of years and ended only about 40 years ago. Millions of Black people were enslaved or ruled over by White nations. The slave owners and rulers always feared that the Black men, in particular, would rise up and revolt against their situation. So they made sure that this did not happen by constantly portraying Black people – especially men and boys –

as mad, bad or dangerous. And White people as naturally superior, stronger, more intelligent and better at everything. Today, most people are better educated and know that this idea of supremacy is rubbish. Most are ashamed of slavery and the White empires that brought misery to large parts of the world. But it is still very easy to see the remains of these beliefs. If you tell Black people they are inferior often enough some will start to believe it; and if White people are told over hundreds of years that they are superior the vast majority will believe it.

It takes time for these beliefs, this culture, to die out. While it is dying Black and mixed parentage boys, especially, will find some White folk showing disrespect.

(Taken from Kirklees LEA video 'Black & White and Aiming High' for Years 6–10)

It is apparent to most commentators (e.g. Gillborn and Mirza 2000) that class and gender combine with ethnic culture to produce a dizzying cocktail of constantly varying factors that help to determine achievement. Although they quite rightly point out that 'the gender gap is considerably smaller than the inequalities of attainment associated with ethnic origin and social class background', it may be that some of the answers to closing the gender gap will also help to address issues associated with class and ethnicity. We shall be exploring that later.

The dangers of stereotyping

We have already discussed the dangers of stereotyping in terms of being lulled into an easy acceptance of pre-determination of learning styles based on gender. The educational community is in danger of making the same mistakes within the fields of class and ethnicity. This can sometimes be the result of intended beneficence or positive discrimination, but actually amounts to having low expectations of some ethnic groups and people from some postal codes, which the data suggest are deprived. We should not decide that all kids from *that* housing estate or with *that* ethnicity will be struggling and need extra help until we know more about them.

3 Writing a whole-school strategy to address under-achievement

> The philosophers have only interpreted the world in various ways; the point is to change it.
>
> (Karl Marx, *Theses on Feuerbach*)

Introduction

This is not a Marxist book but we do think that his argument is pertinent which is why, in some ways, this is the most important chapter of the whole book. This may seem surprising as it is the next three in which you will find the practical and effective strategies that we feel will help raise boys' achievement. Our experience of working in the field, however, strongly suggests that schools are not really short of ideas and actions to address the issue; what they often find difficult is constructing a coherent and manageable plan. Over the past few years there have been hundreds of courses and conferences all over the United Kingdom about the raising of boys' achievement but, as Chapter 1 showed, the impact of these has been largely negligible.

The careful management of change is a critical factor in planning the success of raising boys' achievement. In this chapter we will be marrying the general theory of how to bring about change in education, based on work by authors such as Fullan, Wood and West-Burnham, with the strategy which we have developed in Kirklees which is specifically geared towards raising boys' achievement.

Managing change in the context of boys' achievement

The management of change has increasingly dominated educational management since the late 1980s. It has largely been a bloody, unsatisfactory experience with head teachers and their senior colleagues trying to implement a plethora of externally imposed initiatives. Worthy and progressive as many of these schemes are, we feel they have in some cases given change a bad name and have hindered schools' organic development.

Raising the achievement of boys gives schools the opportunity to recapture control of the management of change. The government has decided that it would be inappropriate to organise a national initiative to raise boys' achievement, partially because it is aware of the 'initiative overload' and partially because it feels that some of its other national initiatives (see Chapter 4) will have a beneficial effect upon boys. This means that schools are largely free to do what *they* think would be appropriate to raise boys' achievement. Our experience suggests that in many cases such change is relatively minor, needing more 'tweaking' of practice than wholesale revolution. This is an important point for the change manager: you are not devaluing or debunking previous practice, merely suggesting reflection and adjustment. Table 3.1 lists arguments that could be put to colleagues (heads, teachers, governors) about the benefits of the school devising its own strategy to raise boys' achievement. Different points may be more persuasive with different types of stakeholders, e.g. teachers interested in equal opportunities *may* be more interested in that perspective than an influential governor who is very keen on meeting targets.

Table 3.1 Reasons why the school should address boys' under-achievement

* The school will find it very difficult to achieve its long-term academic targets without effectively addressing boys' achievement: the girls alone cannot do it.
* The under-achievement of boys significantly contributes to the under-achievement of some girls – through classroom disruption, anti-academic atmosphere and teacher-time diverted by the need to manage boys' behaviour.
* Under-achievement of any pupil is, in itself, a minor tragedy and worthy of action; under-achievement of a cohort of boys stores up problems for the future as they become frustrated and misanthropic members of society and the local community.
* Getting the school experience for boys largely gets it right for all (see 'Introduction' to this book).
* The school can write its own strategy that will meet its own needs.
* The experience of a whole-school ownership and management of change will encourage reflective practice and increase confidence.

In Figure 3.1 we suggest a series of stages that might be considered when planning change.

(a) *Define scale and scope.* What is the scale of the under-achievement? How close are we to the national gender difference? How do we compare with like schools? How long has it been going on? What is it that the school wants to address? All key stages? Who should be involved – all teachers, all staff?

(b) *Establish the team.* Who is interested in this? Who *should* be involved in this? Who is effective in working on projects? Who would rightly see it as good experience and career development? How can we ensure it has

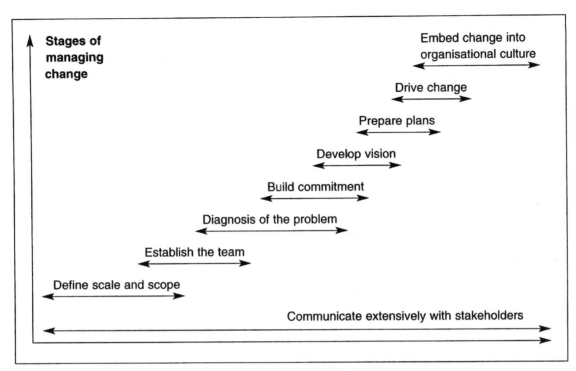

Figure 3.1 Stages of managing change

ongoing support and commitment from the senior management team? Have we got the right balance on the team – creators, persuaders, grafters, organisers, finishers – and are they from the right areas of school?

(c) *Diagnosis of the problem.* What do we think has caused this situation in school? (Use ideas in Chapter 2 as a starting point for discussion.) Does the data suggest that under-achievement is worse in certain areas or year groups? Can we ask each subject area/year group to diagnose the situation in their own area to help widen ownership of the issue? Have we got an anti-swot culture (see Chapter 4)? Can we ask the pupils/school council to consider the issue? Could we use a questionnaire to ascertain what pupils feel about school (see Appendices 3.1A and 3.1B at end of this chapter)?

(d) *Build commitment.* Shall we organise some staff time to discuss the issue and gain support – a training half day? A twilight? Heads of Department meeting? Do we need to prepare for this first by having meetings in subjects/key stages/years? Shall we present our perception of the issue to the governing body? Do we need a governor on the team? Can we present the issue to parents, always remembering the importance of language (see later in this chapter)? What is the most effective and politic sequence of these actions?

(e) *Develop vision.* How do we – the members of the wider school community – literally *see* what we want to achieve? If we took a series of still photographs of our success what would they look like? How do we get a shared vision with the rest of the school community? Discussion, newsletters, meetings, website, letters home?

(f) *Prepare plans.* Are we using the Three Part Strategy (see below)? Have we prepared a detailed action plan (see pro-forma, Appendix 3.2 at end of this chapter)? Has the whole school been consulted about it? Do they own it? Does everybody know their role? Is it properly resourced? Are the targets/performance indicators SMART (specific, measurable, achievable, relevant and time-limited)? Have targets been set for the whole school/different subjects to raise the achievement of boys?

(g) *Drive change.* Does everybody know how and when to start their actions? Who is in charge of ensuring it is done? Have we got the head teacher's or SMT's (Senior Management Team's) support in driving change? How can we lead by example? Are all aware of the deadlines? Are all aware of the monitoring strategy we have agreed to adopt?

(h) *Embed change into organisational culture.* How is the intended change written into the monitoring strategy? Do we need to adjust our classroom observation sheets to include the change? Have all departments/subject areas/year teams got the issue as a standing item on their agendas? Do they feel accountable for their actions for this initiative? Are they clear about their targets? Have they got milestone targets? Are we clear how we are going to celebrate success when these are reached? Have we got targets *we* intend to achieve as a team?

Skills of the change manager

- Vision and enthusiasm for the overall goal
- Ability to listen seriously
- Taking comments seriously – not personally
- Communicating frequently and widely
- Maintaining momentum on key issues
- Building alliances and support
- Tracking and celebrating progress
- Alertness to wider situation and ability to adapt

Barriers to change

- Lack of time
- Too many priorities
- Conflicting initiatives
- Opposition by key persons
- Fear of losing what works well
- Fear of the unknown
- No tradition of challenge and development
- Benefits not apparent
- Low morale
- Anticipating aspects of culture will be dislodged
- Non-recognition of the need for change
- Lack of skill to effect change

The Three Part Strategy

In working closely with schools on raising boys' achievement over the past few years we have been careful to avoid being over-prescriptive about the strategies which they should use. Schools, staff and pupils differ from place to place and have to make up their own mind in the light of what they feel would work. Where we have been very prescriptive, however, is in insisting upon the adoption of the Three Part Strategy. Schools that have ignored it have invariably lost their way or have achieved far less than would otherwise have been the case. The Three Part Strategy consists of raising awareness, macro (whole-school) policies and micro (classroom management) practices.

Raising awareness

Some commentators have argued that this is the *only* thing that schools need to do. Once everybody knows the issues they will automatically adjust their behaviour and the situation will have been effectively addressed. It shows a touching faith in human nature and cites the HIV/AIDS awareness campaign as an example of where this has worked. It conveniently forgets the plethora of other social and medical ills about which most of us are only too aware but in which behaviour has changed very little, such as smoking. We feel that much more has to be done to effectively raise achievement, but that raising awareness is an essential first step. If teachers, parents and the pupils themselves are unaware of the issues they will be reluctant or puzzled participants in any of the macro or micro strategies we describe later. They may resent or even refuse to implement the changes. It is axiomatic in the successful management of change that people have to recognise the need, and that the measures adopted by the institution are seen as clearly appropriate in bringing effective change about.

Raising awareness of teaching staff

Many teaching staff are already only too well aware that boys are an issue. It is boys who tend to be disruptive in lessons, boys who are more often excluded from school and boys who over-populate the least able sets. Nonetheless there is a job to be done with teachers in understanding boys as learners, how and why some under-achieve and what teachers can do about it. In short, teachers are too often concerned about boys' behaviour and need to think about them more in terms of achievement.

There are a number of ways in which this can be done. An examination of SATs and GCSE results by gender will, in most schools, throw up discrepancies of achievement. In the era when most teachers are aware of targets to be reached by the school, faculty and subject, the need to raise boys' achievement will soon become paramount. Otherwise schools will simply not reach the targets being set them by the government and their local education authority: it is a matter of basic arithmetic. Teachers obviously also need to think carefully about the contribution they can make in raising the awareness of those around them – pupils, parents and colleagues – and challenge them to participate in the wider campaign to raise achievement. Teachers may need a course/seminar about the issue of raising boys' achievement. Schools could run some high profile INSET (In-Service Education and Training) as a way into the issue. This may be possible to arrange through the LEA, the local university or from freelance trainers. Many smaller schools, or whole pyramids, have joined forces and financed a training day in order to achieve economies of scale.

Raising awareness of support staff

By 'support staff' we mean all those people who work in schools who are not teachers. They are often called 'non-teaching' staff, but this term is inappropriate. It seems odd to define somebody's role by what they do not do (would teachers enjoy being called 'non-admin staff'?), and at the same time suggests that these staff have no role to play in learning. Classroom assistants, special needs assistants and some technicians are often directly involved in pupils' learning. Clerical staff, lunchtime supervisors, cleaners, caretakers and kitchen staff may have better relationships with some pupils than the teachers do – and have more meaningful conversations with them. Being local, some of them are often the mothers, aunts, grannies and neighbours of the pupils at the school. They all need to know what the problem is. It may be difficult, although not always impossible, to arrange an awareness-raising course for them so a different way may have to be found. Leaflets that illustrate the problem in both national and school terms would be very useful. In primary schools they could be given insights about the topics being taught and the sorts of conversations with the pupils that would reinforce classroom learning. In secondary schools they should be encouraged to talk to the boys about the world of work, the roles of men and how educational success and life after school are linked.

Raising awareness of parents

We feel that the involvement of parents is one of the keys to success in this whole question, as perhaps is the case with nearly all educational problems. Chapter 5 deals with parents in more detail. It is particularly important in the primary school, which may be surprising to some as it is the primary school which generally enjoys much more parental support than the secondaries. A closer look at this support, however, reveals that it is to some extent unsatisfactory and compounds the problem of boys' under-achievement. The vast majority of parents who work voluntarily in school are mothers, which is no bad thing in itself but underscores the lack of a male role model. Furthermore, there is ample evidence that parents tend to expect less from their sons until they reach secondary schools, by which time it is often too late. At the age of eight, after the Key Stage 1 SATs, parents often spend less time reading to their children and hearing their children read. Boys are often not opposed when they choose to 'play out' rather than read a book. We are not advocating the incarceration of boys while parents force-feed them Enid Blyton – reading has to be seen as enjoyable and rewarding – but we are arguing for a balance which parents are well placed to provide. Parents need to be given much clearer guidelines about how they can help their children, not just with reading (see end of chapter note 1), but also with writing, numbers and the application of these in other areas of the curriculum and in everyday life. Level 2 readers, be they girls or boys, with hundred word vocabularies are far from being secure in their skills. They need careful development and encouragement over the next four years.

In secondary schools, much more could be made of engaging parents to raise achievement. It may not be clear to many parents that boys are presently under-achieving and, even when it is, they are not very sure what to do about it other than rather bland appeals to 'work harder', 'revise' or 'do your homework'. Parents often feel disempowered and alienated from the curriculum. The subjects, with the possible exception of English, often seem to be too technical for parents to offer advice to their children. Parents would benefit from each department producing guidelines laying out how parents could help in raising achievement, particularly with boys who are generally less likely to apply themselves. The school, and the various departments, may also wish to consider how homework could be designed to encourage parents to contribute to both its management and completion. Some high schools have introduced a GCSE information evening for parents, which discusses the gender gap and emphasises among other things the need to have high expectations of boys' effort and achievement.

Raising awareness of governors and the wider school community

It is important that the governing body understands the problems which boys are presenting regarding achievement. It may well have to sanction changes in whole-school policy as described later, approve various purchases related to the strategy and be able to respond to parents concerned by the practices the school introduces. Governors should be made aware of the issue by the annual discussion of the SATs and/or GCSE results, but the evidence that this happens is mixed. In some cases governors may wish to form a specific working party, be briefed by the head teacher or an allotted teacher or have the issue regularly discussed on the agenda.

It is useful to have a variety of awareness-raising activities over a period of time so that a rolling programme can be developed, keeping the issue at the forefront of thinking.

Macro (whole-school) policies

Following, or possibly running slightly behind, measures to raise awareness, the management of the school needs to implement strategic, whole-school, plans which are aimed at raising boys' achievement. Perhaps the first step should be to appoint a senior member of staff to coordinate and lead the strategy. He or she may wish to form a working party if there is sufficient interest from staff. Arguably, it is better to use existing structures such as Heads of Department, Senior Management, or Curriculum Coordination meetings. This should ensure that the strategy is not marginalised. It may be better to use both avenues. Whatever the choice, the school needs to ensure that the initiative has clear and accountable leadership and management, and at the same time ensure that everybody in the school sees it is *their* issue. This will be far more secure if staff have been actively involved in the discussions.

Micro (classroom management) strategies

The last section of the Three Part Strategy, but in many ways the most difficult to implement, is that of classroom management, including the choice of teaching styles. These strategies can be adopted by whole departments or year groups, (which we generally recommend), or by individual teachers. In smaller primary schools, the teachers in the whole key stage may wish to discuss whether they are all going to follow a certain strategy. The following are classroom management strategies that will be addressed in Chapters 4 and 6:

- seating policy;
- managing risk-taking behaviour;
- peer work and peer tutoring;
- role models;
- lesson planning and feedback.

None of these strategies should be adopted in isolation from that of the school as a whole, nor before the school has implemented plans to raise the awareness of pupils, parents, staff and governors. In many schools, departments or year groups have decided that they would like to trial some of the ideas. This is likely to be more successful than the isolated teacher striking out on his or her own, unsupported by colleagues, misunderstood by parents and finding it difficult to justify individual behaviour.

Supporting the strategy through monitoring and evaluating the process

Monitoring is not easy. It is particularly difficult in education when there are so many other variables at play. An obvious form of evaluation is by an analysis of the exam results. After all, the whole point of the project is that it is intended to raise boys' achievement. There are some important milestones, however, to be passed before that stage is reached. If evaluation comes only at the end of what may be a three year strategy, and you have not succeeded, what do you do? Will you know what has gone wrong? Table 3.2 sets out some questions which you may like to consider, with suggested time spans from the start of the strategy together with methods of gathering the data.

Obviously there is much more to do in terms of monitoring and evaluation than this. The strategy itself should have in place performance indicators and evaluation methods. The purpose of Table 3.2 is to act as a checklist for management, as an encouragement to support the strategy and the colleagues implementing it.

Note
1. 'Paired Reading' – a video for parents giving them explicit instructions how to read with their children, available from Kirklees LEA, The Deighton Centre, Deighton Road, Huddersfield HD2 1JP Tel 01484 225793.

Table 3.2 Supporting and monitoring the strategy

Action and Key Questions	Time	Method
1. Have you a clearly written strategy which all staff and governors have been involved in/briefed on? Do you know *your* boys? Are you aware of how *your* boys are performing in school? Are they performing in line with expectations: look at input data like NFER tests or SATs. Are you aware how *your* boys are responding to schooling? Have you got data about level of involvement in school activities or pastoral problems? Where are the successful boys in your school? Are pupils/students aware of the issue of boys' under-achievement?	After 3 months.	By staff meeting. By pupil questionnaire or form tutorials.
2. Are parents aware of the issues?	After 3 months.	By meetings. By newsletters. By homework diary/planner. By parental questionnaire
3. Have you set in place a management structure of the strategy which staff recognise? Are systems in place in the school which ensure the embedding of the strategies and addressing of the issue in 'normal' school life?	After 3 months. After 1 year. After 18 months.	By meetings. By professional interviews or appraisal.
4. Have the macro strategies in school got clear leadership and SMART (specific, measurable, achievable, relevant and time-limited) targets?	After 3 months. After 1 year. After 2 years.	By discussion. By whole-staff discussion.
5. Have the micro strategies received sufficient encouragement and support from school management? What is being learned from early trials? Has there been any observation of micro strategies in operation? Have teachers watched each other in these strategies and fed back their observations?	After 3 months. After 6 months. After 9 months, etc. Every 3 months.	Discussion with Heads of Department. Teachers observe good practice. Discussion with teachers (they have to know that the SMT really care about what they are doing).
6. Have you established some sort of baseline for assessing progress, such as: boys' (and girls') enjoyment of school; enjoyment of specific subjects (could be controversial!); attendance; parental attitude to school; number of boys/girls reported for behavioural reasons; number of boys/girls recommended for effort rewards; punctuality to lessons; SATs results (tied to CATs (Cognitive Abilities Tests) scores – in secondary schools) GCSE results (as above).	After 3 months. Then yearly.	By questionnaire. By examination of school records. By listening to pupils.

Appendix 3.1A

To be completed by the teacher:

Key Stage 1
QUESTIONNAIRE ABOUT SCHOOL

No talking. No looking at anyone else's paper.
Do NOT put your name on this paper. It is strictly anonymous.

Year Group

Girl   *(PLEASE RING)*   **Boy**

1. Do you generally enjoy coming to school? *(Please tick)*

    Yes   No

2. Write or draw what you like best about school?

3. Write or draw what you like least about school?

4. How do you feel if your teacher is **pleased** with your work? *(Please tick one face)*

5. How do feel if your teacher is **not pleased** with your work? *(Please tick one face)*

6. Are you pleased with your work? *(Please tick one face)*

Yes   No

7. Is your head teacher pleased with your work? *(Please tick one face)*

Yes   No   Don't know

8. Who works best in class? *(Please tick one figure)*

Boys   Girls

9. Which two things do you **most enjoy** in school? *(Tick two of the boxes below)*

Writing ❑   Reading ❑   Art ❑   PE ❑

40

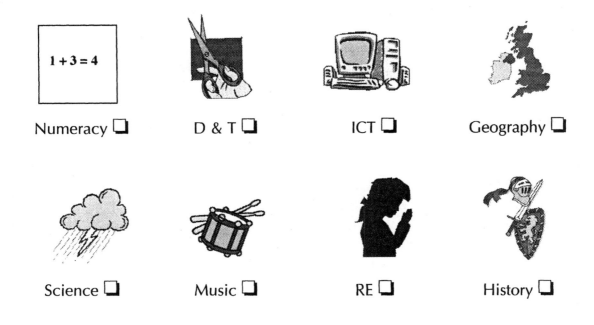

Numeracy ❑   D & T ❑   ICT ❑   Geography ❑

Science ❑   Music ❑   RE ❑   History ❑

10. Which subject do you **dislike** the most? *(Tick two of the boxes below)*

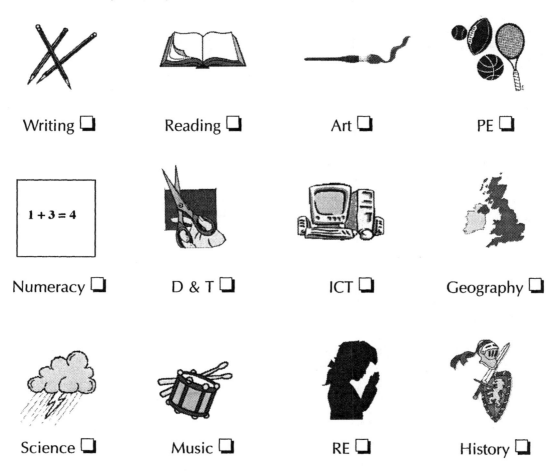

Writing ❑   Reading ❑   Art ❑   PE ❑

Numeracy ❑   D & T ❑   ICT ❑   Geography ❑

Science ❑   Music ❑   RE ❑   History ❑

11. What do you think boys are good at? *(Tick two of the boxes below)*

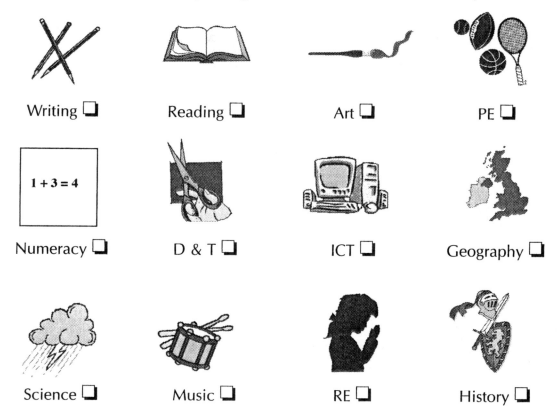

12. What do you think girls are good at? *(Tick two of the boxes below)*

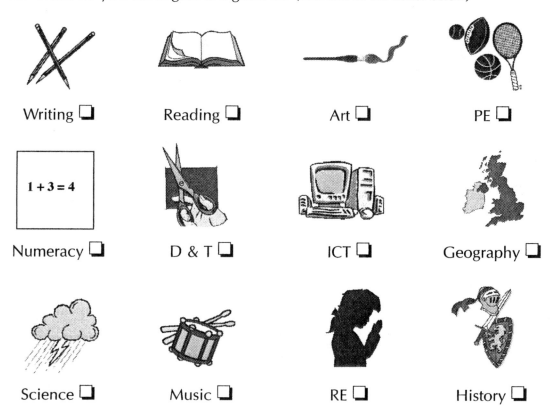

13. Do you think your teacher likes you? *(Please tick one face)*

Yes

No

14. How do you know?

15. Do you like working? *(Please tick one)*

   (a) By yourself   ❑

   (b) In a pair   ❑

   (c) In a group   ❑

   (d) With the whole class ❑

Appendix 3.1B

To be completed by the teacher:

Key Stage 2
QUESTIONNAIRE ABOUT SCHOOL

No talking. No looking at anyone else's paper.
Do NOT put your name on this paper. It is strictly anonymous.

Year Group

Girl　　　　　　　　　*(PLEASE RING)*　　　　　　　　　**Boy**

1. Do you enjoy coming to school?

　　Yes　　No　　Sometimes　　Never　　*(Please ring one)*

2. What do you like best at school?

3. What do you like least at school?

4. Do you expect to get into trouble? *(Please ring one answer)*

　　(a) Every day　　　　　　　(c) Hardly ever

　　(b) Some days　　　　　　　(d) Never

5. Do you look forward to lunchtimes? *(Please ring one answer)*

　　(a) Every day　　　　　　　(c) Hardly ever

　　(b) Some days　　　　　　　(d) Never

6. Do you get into trouble at lunchtimes? *(Please ring one answer)*

　　(a) Every day　　　　　　　(c) Hardly ever

　　(b) Some days　　　　　　　(d) Never

7. How do you feel if your teacher is pleased with your work? *(You can ring more than one answer)*

   (a) Happy   (b) Proud   (c) Embarrassed   (d) Fine   (e) Not bothered

8. How do feel if your teacher is **not** pleased with your work? *(You can ring more than one answer)*

   (a) Unhappy   (b) Upset   (c) Embarrassed   (d) Fine   (e) Not bothered

9. When you are working in lessons, if you get anything wrong how does it make you feel? *(Please ring one answer)*
   (a) That you will try harder
   (b) That you will give up
   (c) Not bothered

10. Are you proud of your work? *(Please ring one)*

    (a) Every day   (b) Some days   (c) Hardly ever   (d) Never

11. Is your head teacher proud of your work? *(Please ring one)*

    (a) Yes   (b) No   (c) Don't know

12. Who works best in class? *(Please ring one)*

    (a) Boys   (b) Girls   (c) Both

13. What are boys good at?

14. What are girls good at?

15. Do you like working? *(Please number 1 to 4 in order of preference, 1 = best, 4 = worst)*
    (a) By yourself   ❏   (c) In a group   ❏
    (b) In a pair   ❏   (d) With the whole class ❏

16. Which two subjects do you most enjoy in school? *(Tick two only)*

    Science ❏ English – reading ❏ English – writing ❏ Mathematics ❏
    Geography ❏ History ❏ Music ❏ Art ❏ PE ❏ RE ❏ ICT ❏

17. Why do you enjoy these two subjects?

18. Which two subjects do you **dislike** the most? *(Tick two only)*

    Science ❏ English – reading ❏ English – writing ❏ Mathematics ❏
    Geography ❏ History ❏ Music ❏ Art ❏ PE ❏ RE ❏ ICT ❏

19. Why do you dislike these two subjects?

20. Do you think your teacher likes you? *(Please ring one answer)*

    (a) Always   (b) Usually   (c) Sometimes   (d) Never

21. How do you know?

APPENDIX 3.2

A pro-forma on which to base an action plan

Task	Who?	When?	Resources	Success Criteria	Progress/ monitoring	Priority

4 Practical whole-school strategies

Strategies to raise the achievement of under-achieving boys, boys in minority ethnic groups and boys disadvantaged by class

The government's existing and projected strategies

In February 2001, the government, although concerned by the reported under-achievement of some boys, decided against a specific initiative or intervention to address the situation (Noble 2001). The reasons for this were that schools were already groaning under the accumulated yoke of initiatives, and also because it was felt that some of the government's existing policies would eventually address the situation. These included:

(a) The National Literacy Strategy in primary schools. The government was much encouraged by the gender gap in English falling from 16 percentage points difference in 1998 to 9 points difference in 2000 (see Chapter 1). It was felt that the structure of the literacy hour, with its focus, variety of texts and different activities was having a beneficial effect upon boys.

(b) The diminution of class sizes at Key Stage 1 (nearly all classes were reduced to 30 or less between 1998–2001) was probably beneficial to both genders, but particularly boys who often find early schooling more traumatic (see Chapter 2) and need more teacher time.

(c) The expected benefits of the 'roll-out' of the Key Stage 3 strategy, particularly the extension of the National Literacy Strategy to 11–14 year olds and the intended teaching and learning 'revolution' across the curriculum. The Key Stage 3 SATs results in English had been very disappointing in 1999 and 2000, especially for boys, and the government felt that higher achievement at Key Stage 2 would bring higher expectation, especially when combined with the new strategy.

(d) The introduction of the 'Excellence In Cities' and 'Excellence In Clusters' strategies in which targeted resources were put into the very geographical areas in which boys were doing worst, although not aimed specifically at boys. These highly centralised interventions involved, among other things, the use of paid learning mentors and learning support units inside schools.

(e) The rolling introduction of the new Connexions Service between 2001 and 2003, which is also aimed to supply learning mentors and more tailored guidance for 13–18 year olds from an amalgam of the existing careers service , youth service, youth justice and other services.

(f) The authority for schools to 'disapply' parts of the National Curriculum for some students at Key Stage 4, and instead provide a more appropriate range of activities that answer the student's growing need for relevance to the next stage of his or her life.

(g) The gradual evolution of GNVQ courses in secondary schools, particularly for 14–16 year olds, that would be more appropriate for the more vocationally minded.

It is impossible at this stage to know whether these would be sufficient to address boys' achievement effectively. Much of it seems very worthy and well-considered but its level of success is pure conjecture. We do have some concerns about certain aspects of the *application* of these strategies:

1. That there is no overall, binding theme throughout the programmes that recognises boys' achievement as an issue and presents coherent and consistent strategies to address it, particularly in relation to teaching and learning styles.
2. That the Key Stage 3 Literacy Strategy will not be as well supported by schools as it was in the primary years. It is opposed, for example, by NATE (National Association for the Teachers of English), and secondary teachers tend to be more independently minded than their primary colleagues.
3. That the Connexions Service will not be as well organised nor as seamless as schools and students need.
4. That the learning mentors employed so far are, anecdotally, 66 per cent female and do not accurately represent minority ethnic groups – and that the implications of this have not been properly considered.
5. That some examples of disapplication of the Key Stage 4 curriculum by schools suggest a lack of rigour, structure and monitoring.

Some of these concerns may prove groundless, or merely the teething troubles experienced by any new service or initiative. We hope that they are all successful.

The anti-swot culture

Schools should be aware of any anti-swot culture in their midst. As an indication, nearly all secondary schools have one to a greater or lesser extent and a large number of primary schools are aware of such a culture in Years 5 and 6. It is interesting to reflect that, in school years in which the hard workers are also successful at sport and/or are socially skilled, there tends to be far less of this antagonism. Teachers can usually sense the presence of an anti-swot culture: tell-tale signs are the use of the word 'swot', 'bof', etc., as a term of abuse, even light-heartedly, and the way in which some boys may react to public praise and reward for their work or effort. If they become embarrassed, shun public attention, prefer private praise or even make a point of not coming top – it may mean that an anti-swot culture is in operation. It may, of course, merely mean that they are shy. Most teachers will be able to judge which.

An anti-swot culture is a serious threat to boys' and girls' achievement. Girls are far from immune from it. Although their hard work is more likely to be tolerated by their less enthusiastic peers of both genders, we are aware that some girls have felt intimidated and concerned if they were seen to do too well in class.

Combating the anti-swot culture

We feel that the anti-swot culture should be treated in the same way as racism: that it should never be tolerated. It is a direct attack upon equal opportunities, denigrates the very purpose of school and denies many the chance of fulfilling their potential. The question is what to do about it. The very words 'swot', 'bof', etc., should be banned in school and pupils given the chance to discuss the issues behind such a ban. Some staff, also, need to be sure that they are not encouraging an anti-swot culture, even subconsciously. For example, unpublished research in secondary schools by Worcestershire Health Authority strongly suggests that the image projected by the PE department had a very strong effect upon pupils' experience and liking of school. Heavily traditional, macho and competitive departments tended to encourage a narrow, exclusive and intolerant view of manhood in which many boys felt uncomfortable, but had to play along with. Departments which portrayed men as being caring, listening, cooperative and inclusive tended to generate a culture in which boys felt less pressured to conform to a stereotype and more accepted for what they wanted to be.

Schools can also address the anti-swot culture in a direct, whole-school fashion. Some schools in Kirklees have organised boys' conferences in which a special emphasis was put on how boys could challenge the anti-swot culture in school. In one school, this has led to *pupils* writing materials for PSHE for Years 8 and 9 addressing the work ethic.

Experience of attempts to change attitudes elsewhere suggests that success is far more likely if the message is positive rather than negative. Although there should be a 'zero tolerance' of anti-swot remarks in the classroom and school in general, school managers have to think about the culture they are trying to encourage. Research by the Institute of Education in London suggested that there are eleven characteristics of effective schools, and two of these are 'a learning environment' and 'a learning organisation'. What should a school do to make sure that it displays itself in this way? When asked why they are at school only a minority of boys will volunteer the answer that they are there to learn. They will readily agree, if pressed, that it is one of their objectives but not the first one that comes to their mind. The need to behave, survive, obey the rules, because their parents make them, because it is the law, to avoid bullies are all reasons volunteered before that of learning. It is the task of schools to make it very clear that the prime purpose pupils attend school is to learn, and that everything that supports that aim will be encouraged. Conversely, anything which detracts from that aim will be strongly discouraged but this should not be a diktat levelled at pupils and their parents by a teaching staff obsessed with government-inspired targets: this simply would not work. It is the responsibility of *all* – perhaps led by the senior management team – to make the school a learning organisation. The Welsh word 'dysgu' is worthy of discussion. It means 'teaching' and 'learning'. The Welsh are not simply short of words and doubling up. It is a profound insight into what schools and teaching should be about. Schools have to *show* that they are learning organisations, not simply tell. This could mean:

- a display of courses and qualifications being undertaken by staff;
- a review of books recently read by staff;
- a display of what staff learned during the holidays;
- classroom discussion of courses and conferences attended by staff;
- display of last year's leavers and what they are doing/what they are learning;
- teachers – and other staff – making it clear that they are continuing to learn, about their subject, about what works in the classroom, about preferred learning styles, about the pupils they teach (we pick up this theme again later in the book when discussing seating plans and shared reading in Chapter 6);
- schools publicly recognising that there are things worth learning that are not reflected in the National Curriculum and league tables and that personal and social development is as important as academic success, e.g. praise in assembly for pupils' hobbies and public spiritedness;
- teachers establishing a climate in which pupils are constantly encouraged to discuss what they have learned, rather than what they have not.

The principles of health promotion have an important point for any anti-swot strategy. Young people, like everybody else, respond much better to positive messages telling them they *can* do and be, than they do to negative exhortations to stop behaviour that we may regard as undesirable. Hence, although our purpose may be to eradicate the anti-swot culture from schools, the path to our objective may lie more with the positive message of championing and modelling the learning school. This can be exemplified in establishing a climate in which pupils are constantly encouraged to discuss what they have learned, rather than what they have not.

Expectations and language

It is a little patronising to discuss the importance of expectation; all teachers acknowledge it and will readily trot out the arguments during any interview, but we still hear huge amounts of negative expectation when teachers, and parents, discuss boys' achievement and behaviour. 'It's a boy-heavy year, so we're struggling to reach our targets'; 'Boys will be boys'; and 'He's not badly behaved, for a boy'. We do not know the extent to which these sometimes subtle, but invariably negative, messages are rehearsed with boys themselves. We do know from our research (Kirklees 2000, unpublished), that boys often expect to be treated in a negative fashion, and differently from girls. Indeed, sexist language against boys is often tolerated or even used by 'liberal' teachers who would not tolerate it the other way around. Schools need to reach a policy and practice that does not support the negative stereotypes of boys that are regularly fed them by the mass media, but instead incessantly tells them that boys – and girls – are hard workers and capable of high achievement in any field that captures their interests and strengths. Errant behaviour and under-achievement should be portrayed as exactly that; atypical of their gender, of themselves and as a danger to the fulfilment of their potential. Contrasting boys to girls in any way will not usually help boys to think of themselves as cooperative, as learners and as achievers.

For similar reasons it is important that when schools raise awareness of the issue of boys' under-achievement, they need to be very careful about the language that is used. If awareness is raised and boys hear from their parents, lunchtime supervisor, education social worker, teachers and lollipop ladies that boys are under-achieving, there is a great danger that they will, *ergo*, under-achieve. They will begin to 'walk the talk' as a definition of being a boy is supplied for them. Instead, they should hear that boys and girls can achieve – and they should see examples of that all around them.

Display

Some schools have display policies; others have practices instead. Very few systematically address the issue of boys' achievement through display. Whatever is shown on the corridors and in classrooms should address these questions:

1. To what extent is the display confirming boys – all boys – and girls as learners?
2. To what extent is it widening choices and opportunities for boys and girls?
3. To what extent is it showing younger boys that one of the characteristics of being an older boy (most boys and girls aspire to being three or four years older than they are – a desire that tends to peter out in the mid to late twenties!) is being a learner?
4. To what extent does the display celebrate the achievement of *all* boys in the school?
5. To what extent does the display capture the achievement of boys from a variety of cultures, and reflect aspects of boys' cultures both from the school community and also globally?

All these questions may well mean schools end up having a display rota that values the work of every pupil, has a 'where are they now?' board of immediately past pupils, and employs good quality images of boys, men, girls and women from a variety of backgrounds in a variety of occupations and professions. Displays need to change reasonably rapidly to maintain effect and be supported by references in class, assembly and communications with parents.

Ethos

The ethos of a school is very hard to define and measure. It is often determined by the management style and effectiveness of the head teacher, but there are a number of other variables – attitude of staff, workload, resources, class sizes – that will impact upon the ethos of a school and the degree to which boys feel comfortable, stimulated and eager to learn. In a school that was determined to build an ethos that would help boys, one would expect to see:

- a well understood and consistently applied system for rewarding good behaviour and effort, and for dealing with discipline problems;
- a supportive proactive, pastoral system in which pupils are actively encouraged to reflect on their needs and progress;
- an active, elected and representative school and/or year council;
- pupils encouraged to take and accept responsibility within all subjects and within all years;
- a varied programme of extracurricular activities available to all pupils;
- a strong element of vertical activity (i.e. older pupils working with younger ones) in the school;
- a strong, well-publicised and supported moral code with equality of opportunity and social inclusion to the fore;
- a welcome given to parents/carers and the wider school community to come into school to support activities;
- a willingness to go out and meet the school community *in* the community;
- a determination to praise, far more than condemn, in all aspects of school life, in all subjects, in all years and for all pupils.

All of this is, of course, merely good practice. As we said in the Introduction to this book, the pursuit of raising boys' achievement is a window of opportunity to good practice.

The Magic Number Eight

The eight year old

Research (Bleach *et al.* 1998), observation and anecdote strongly suggest that there are two key years which schools need to address if they are to reverse the under-achievement of boys. Eight-year-old boys, or more accurately those in Year 3, and those boys in Year 8 of the secondary school show certain common characteristics. Year 8 of the few existing middle schools is a slightly different issue.

The eight-year-old boy has completed his Key Stage 1 SATs and he has over three years (a lifetime in junior terms) before his next public tests. Moreover, his parents, as discussed in Chapter 5, are less likely to encourage his reading and general work than they did before SATs, and possibly less than they do his sister.

Added to this is the often less than interesting, very overcrowded and too content-based Key Stage 2 curriculum. The boy finds·himself having to do more writing, more copying and more reading than seems comfortable. There is also the possibility, although the boy probably would not protest very much, that his teacher is just a little more relaxed about progress than the previous year when the teacher had to get the pupils through SATs and feel very accountable to parents. This new teacher may well feel that his Level 2 in English was a little flattering and probably feels that a period of consolidation is in order. Besides which, there's an awful lot of curriculum to plough through. Just as well, she says to herself, that it's not me that has to get them to Level 4 in four years' time. The momentum of progress is slowed. The girls – who as a cohort tend to be much happier in the repetitive tasks of writing, copying, drawing and presenting well organised, neat work – begin to draw further ahead of the boys. This is, of course, a gross stereotype which is very unfair to thousands of skilful and aware Year 3 teachers – however, it is also a scenario that many teachers recognise. The question is what to do about it. Here are some 'ideas':

- Schools need to be careful to ensure that the texts to be used in the literacy hour are not too heavily weighted towards relationships/emotions/feelings.
- Boys are bored by worksheets. Schools may want to think about how to use them less, or at least more imaginatively (e.g. the more structured worksheets suggested by Geoff Hannon (1997) which help to teach skills in organising ideas) so that individuals within groups take on different but mutually supportive tasks, and to build in elements of challenge, not just completion.
- The literacy hour, with its very structured approach and short-term tasks should help boys disproportionately compared to girls. The plenary session at the end, with its accent on short-term learning achievements and feedback should be particularly helpful to boys if done well.
- It may be a good idea to use Year 3 to have a renewed blitz on parents, supplying them with a specially written leaflet about the issue and their role in continuing to encourage reading.
- Use this year, particularly, to invite male role models in to school.
- Ask staff to think about planning short-term, quick-reward learning objectives/challenges for boys and girls.
- Analyse the content of the library or ask the boys themselves to analyse it.
- More controversially and possibly less welcome, schools could decide to undertake the voluntary Year 3 and/or 4 SATs – although what exactly you wish to get out of it should be clear. Merely putting pressure on teachers, pupils and parents is not a very laudable objective. Having clear targets, learning objectives and teaching strategies which the SATs could be used to support is another matter altogether.

The 'annus horribilus' – Year 8 boys

Are Year 8 boys horrible? Traditionally, Year 9 has been the time when boys exhibit most troublesome behaviour in greater numbers, but there are good reasons for regarding Year 8 boys as inhabiting a critical time, when many show the initial tendencies to reject the rules and norms of school and to become more questioning of the worth of learning to them.

In many ways, this is only to be expected. They are no longer the new Year 7 kids on the block. They have a confidence and an understanding of their place in the school institution. They are also more independent of their parents, not just because the maturing process and the hormonal revolution is upon them, making peer approval often more influential than parental pressure, but because at the age of 13 they are more able to find paid part-time employment. It is the age when paper-rounds can legally be undertaken. Year 8 is also the time when many boys – and girls – find themselves setted for the first time. This should not be underestimated. They may have done less well than their peers in the Key Stage 2 SATs, but setting means that many feel that they have officially been recognised as having failed, and as a result they are to receive a different educational experience from their peers.

Barbara Walker's research into boys and young men suggests that boys, much more than girls, are working to build both a public and private self.

> Within their private selves these boys were exploring concepts such as doubt, independence, fear, romance, uncertainty, academic pressure and anxiety – building a personal moral code. Within the group they appeared to be learning solidarity, trust, judgement; learning the banter of affability; learning to be part of a team.
>
> (Quoted in the *TES*, October 1996)

Walker goes on to suggest that the two personae tend to narrow as the boys get older, but for 13 year olds it is very important that the public front is accepted and supported. Schools do not always recognise the nature of boys' development and sometimes try to oppose or suppress its manifestations rather than to channel its energies. Kevan Bleach (Bleach *et al.* 1998) has suggested that the boys' changes in attitude in Year 8 are substantially rooted in educational challenges, the quality of teaching and the nature of pupil–teacher relationships. What is crucial about Year 8 is that if boys do adopt a public scepticism towards learning and academic achievement at this age it is very difficult for them to change back in time to affect their school career.

A Norfolk head teacher, when asked to explain why his GCSE results consistently showed boys achieving as well as girls commented 'I talk to my Year 8 Boys'. He did more than talk to them. The following is a list of possible ways of keeping Year 8 boys interested and alert to academic success. It is not rocket science, and reflects some of the things we have discussed before.

1. Encourage/insist that teachers in Year 8 provide a variety of active learning experiences, and agree a regime for monitoring this and learning effective practice between colleagues. Practical investigations, oral work, quizzes, challenges, group work and role play are much more interesting, and will capture peer group approval.
2. Focus even more closely on literacy. Have visiting, male readers, writers-in-

residence, book weeks, library competitions. Ask Year 8 boys to review the library and make recommendations for change. Use ICT to encourage word processing and better presentation. Place more value on non-fiction and science fiction, magazines and comics. Ask students to share their books. Ask them to score books and compare the marks given.

3. Design homework so that it involves boys working in pairs or groups on active or investigative work. Try to design homework that helps the students to practise the skills learned in the classroom, but avoid setting work that is merely completion of work started in class.

4. Think carefully about the way the school praises boys. Is it generally public or private? What sort of praise do boys prefer? Has the school got an *effective* reward system in place and how do Year 8 boys respond to it? Celebrate achievement in display, of both individuals and of teams.

5. Introduce mentoring, possibly targeted at boys who staff feel are particularly at risk of losing motivation. (See later section in this chapter on mentoring.)

6. Establish exciting events to anticipate and enjoy, and which are connected to learning, e.g. skiing trips (do schools connect this sufficiently to learning?), field trips, exchange visits, historical primary evidence gathering.

7. Introduce the Internet, e-mail and ICT as important tools to learn through, not as an enjoyable off-task addition to 'real' or 'normal' learning.

The general message has to be that Year 8 boys are in need of a specially vigilant eye, and that as they embrace adolescence with its peer pressure and questioning of previously accepted authority, the school has to move to a culture which accepts the development and seeks ways to work with it.

Curriculum materials

Schools should be able to set themselves the task of reflecting on their curriculum materials and asking themselves the questions:

(a) How visually attractive are these to boys? Do they portray boys doing things? Are they bright, engaging and/or interesting? Do they look as if they would connect to the real lives led by boys of the age in question?

(b) Are the activities suggested or demanded by the materials likely to appeal to under-achieving boys' preferred learning styles? In other words, do they demand a variety of active learning styles? Do they give the opportunity to learn socially with others? (These questions will be explored again in Chapter 6.)

(c) Do the materials portray boys as doers, learners and achievers in a variety of activities? Do they expand boys' potential view of themselves or diminish them?

(d) Are the materials culturally appropriate? Do they show boys from different sorts of ethnic and class backgrounds as learners? Is there celebration of different festivals and culturally identifying events from all over the world?

(e) Is the language appropriate for the ability and maturity of the pupils in the class?

An interesting exercise is to ask different subject teams (in secondary schools) or year or key stage teams in primary schools to take these questions and investigate another subject/year/key stage. A more detached eye is usually in a better position to judge than colleagues who are using the materials all the time. This exercise has to be carefully prepared with well-rehearsed ground rules about constructive criticism in order to avoid the danger of offence being given and taken.

An alternative exercise is to simply ask the same questions of the pupils themselves, or to get the school council to investigate the issue.

Curriculum content

In many ways, schools can do very little about the content of the curriculum. The National Curriculum has to be taught and the SATs and GCSEs league tables are an expression of the government's commitment to judge schools' effectiveness in doing so – however, the curriculum is not quite so inflexible as it once was. The major change has come in secondary schools. History, geography, art and music are no longer statutory at Key Stage 4. The advent of GNVQs in Key Stage 4 has presented schools with an option that helps some of its otherwise under-achieving pupils. GNVQs have an emphasis on activity and preparation for the world of work and some students can see a direct link with their employment and career aspirations that may not have been so obvious in French or mathematics. Similarly, secondary schools can now have students disapplied from other parts of the National Curriculum, specifically design and technology and modern foreign languages, and this again introduces flexibility into a system that was previously experiencing the great strain of insisting on an inappropriate curriculum for many boys, and girls.

The question is: what can schools do with this extra flexibility? It should vary depending on the needs of the students: some will need extra tuition in the core subjects; others can follow a GNVQ course; some will be able to spend time in the local tertiary college; others can have extended work experience, follow a key skills course or an accredited personal development course like ASDAN (Award Scheme Development and Accreditation Network).

In the other key stages, there is far less scope for flexibility. Primary schools have the option of introducing a foreign language in Key Stage 2, which a few are doing, but it is unlikely to address the need of under-achieving boys. The main benefit for 5–14-year-old boys in the Curriculum 2000 changes will be the enhancement of Personal, Social and Health Education (PSHE) and citizenship. These changes have in most schools yet to make an impact, but the building blocks of statutory requirement (citizenship in Key Stages 3 and 4 from September 2002), more rigorous inspection of PSHE by OFSTED and the support available from the National Healthy School Standard (NHSS) are in place. They offer schools a chance to make education more inclusive, more reflective and for boys to really address the question of what it means to be a man, and the type of culture they would really want in school to help them learn. One south London school has used the NHSS in just this way to successfully tackle bullying and anti-swottism in the school.

Mentoring

Mentoring is a fairly new addition to the strategies at a school's disposal and it can take a number of forms. The idea of mentoring is that the student has a regular discussion about his or her learning with a significant other, with whom he or she can share problems, ideas, and progress. Just what sort of mentoring a school chooses is largely a matter of resources as much as educational principle. Another problem is deciding exactly who should be mentored. Some schools have chosen 'twelve students of concern' in each year after consulting year tutors or class teachers. Others have decided to concentrate on certain year groups, and some ensure that all boys and girls get access to it. In secondary schools, Year 11 is often targeted for mentoring because of the proximity of the GCSEs, although there is plenty of evidence that this effort could be better spent in Year 8 (see above). Suggestions for content and structure of mentoring sessions and how they can be organised are described below. Don't be afraid initially to mentor on a small scale: the key is that it must be manageable and sustained.

(a) Mentoring by the senior management team and/or all teachers

The coverage and depth of any mentoring scheme will depend on the number of staff a school has available. Some schools are reaching the conclusion that all form tutors in the secondary school must become mentors. This has sometimes meant that the PSE curriculum that they used to teach has had to be picked up by subjects or by a timetabled block. The form tutor's main task becomes much more specific. He or she is the academic mentor for all the students in the form. This involves a highly structured and well-supported schedule in which students are interviewed on a regular basis, either alone or in carefully chosen pairs. The interview has to be supported by information or reports from subject teachers. The interview may start with the sort of general questions such as these:

1. How are things going at the moment? Are you enjoying schoolwork more or less than last year?
2. Which subjects are you enjoying most? What is it about those subjects which you enjoy? Which subjects are not going so well? Why is this?
3. Do you understand the work you are doing in each subject? Is the work explained clearly?

4. What is the classroom atmosphere like? Is it friendly? Do you enjoy being there?
5. Are there any individuals or groups who mess about in class and stop you working?
6. Does the teacher tell you how you are getting on?
7. Do you think you are working harder this year than last year? Why do you think that?
8. What would make you work harder than you do now?
9. What do you think this school could do to help boys/girls do better?

Obviously there have to be clearly understood rules concerning the discussion of specific colleagues. This has to be kept on a professional basis if the scheme is going to work. The mentor would also be using the school's statistics regarding NFER/CATs scores and predicted grades (in the older years) to help the student agree academic targets. (See later section on target setting.)

If the mentoring is undertaken by only a fraction of the staff, possibly the senior team, the school will have to be more selective about the students it wants to see. It may want to think about the following as possible cohorts:

1. Year 11 boys and/or girls.
2. Year 11 boys and/or girls who are suspected of under-achieving.
3. Year 8 boys and/or girls who are under-achieving.
4. Boys and/or girls from all years who are under-achieving.
5. Boys and/or girls from all years who are seen as 'culture-setters', those whose opinions and behaviour often lead others.

With the imminent introduction of the Connexions Service in many areas and the growth of 'Excellence In Cities' and 'Excellence In Clusters' many more pupils should be accessing mentoring from outside the school. This is potentially very beneficial for boys but – as mentioned at the beginning of the chapter – it is very important that mentors have the respect and confidence of the boys involved. This may have implications for the age, attitude, ethnicity and gender of the mentors.

(b) Peer mentoring

The idea of peer mentoring is that it is more time efficient than that done by teachers; that peers can effectively continue the mentoring in their own time if they wish; and that the language and discussion may be more comfortable and meaningful to the students. If, however, it is seen by teachers merely as a method by which responsibility is passed to the students it will not work. The school has to value the system, and show that it values it. This means that a great deal of investment has to be put into its planning, preparation of teachers and training of students. Students should be involved in the planning of it; it should not be something that happens *to* them. Students should be asked to pick a mentor who is not from their normal cohort of close friends. It would be helpful to both genders if they had to choose someone of the opposite sex. This would give them an opportunity to understand the thinking of their opposites, and would also expose them to a more critical exposé than might otherwise be the case. In some schools mentoring has been one way, with older students mentoring younger ones, while other schools have chosen horizontally paired mentoring where the partners mentor each other. There are a number of variations which schools will want to consider and trial.

(c) Industrial mentoring

In some areas, particularly in Norfolk LEA, schools have established partnerships with local businesses – factories, offices, banks, etc. – in which male employees have come in to school to work as mentors for boys, particularly under-achieving boys. This partnership has a number of benefits. The boys, who in some cases may lack an adult male role model, get the chance to talk to a male – who is not a teacher – about the world of work, its disciplines and its benefits. He can also see how he may be in a few years' time. It gives him a longer-term perspective which is not easily dismissed. The mentor may talk to him about the questions listed above, about his targets and about his ambitions outside school. Businesses are usually quite happy for their staff to become involved. They view it as a form of personal development and of establishing a meaningful relationship with the local community. In some places, particularly with primary schools, the mentor is more of a reader or a listener of reading. In all cases, using outside mentors throws up questions of child protection and of training. Both these require time and effort but they should not be barriers to what can be a very rewarding experience for all involved. In the case of child protection, cooperation will be needed from the police who will have to interrogate criminal records. Policy may vary between forces, or even between divisions within the same force, so it may be wise to seek political support via the Chief Constable or the Chair of the Police Authority. This support may be more likely if the local Police themselves are involved in the mentoring. The appropriateness of this will vary enormously depending on age of the pupils, local attitudes to the Police and the suitability of individual officers.

Use of prior attainment measures

Schools have never been so rich in data about pupils, and this has engendered a culture that is taken sometimes to the point of *ad tedium* and occasionally to *ad nauseam*. Baseline profiles, SATs at Key Stages 1, 2 and 3 all give information about what pupils have previously achieved and therefore, what they might be capable of achieving in the future. We might hope that a pupil who has achieved to national expectations, i.e. Level 2 at 7 years old, Level 4 at 11 years old and Level 5 at 14 years old, might then go on to obtain five or more GCSEs at A*-C grades. It is not a perfect science and it does not happen quite like that.
    The DfEE revealed research in 2001 (DfEE 2001) which showed that:

- 52 per cent of students who achieve Level 5 in English at Key Stage 3 SATs gain 5+ A*-C GCSEs; of the 52 per cent, 60 per cent of girls and 44 per cent of boys achieve 5+ A*-C;

- 93 per cent of students who achieve Level 6 in English at Key Stage 3 SATs gain 5+ A*-C GCSEs; of these, 95 per cent of girls and 90 per cent of boys achieve 5+ A*-C.

It is obvious that even at Key Stage 4, the gender effect is still having an impact on achievement, at an age when, after nine years of schooling, one might suspect that gender had been stripped out of the equation. Some research recently undertaken in a Kirklees high school revealed that none of their latest crop of Oxbridge entrants particularly shone at Key Stage 3. So what we say about using prior attainment carries some very large caveats. We should not try to prophesy the maximum that could be attained by any one pupil, but we may be able to see where pupils are under-achieving and take action based on this analysis.

Target setting

All schools have targets for academic achievement. Whether they be the government inspired targets at Key Stage 2, the number of A*-C passes at GCSE or each subject's or key stage's internally driven targets for their cohort, the age of target setting is upon us, and it is unlikely to go away. The targets set by the government for itself have been translated into targets for each LEA, which in turn have negotiated targets for each of their schools. Many schools, quite naturally, feel that their targets are unfair, too ambitious or just impossible but, like it or not, they will be judged by their success in meeting them.

The principle of subsidiarity, not often used in education, comes into play here. If the government targets depend on LEAs, and the LEAs' targets depend on schools, then the schools' targets depend on individual students. If schools are going to meet their targets, then they have to talk very intensively with their students about their own, individual targets. Most primary schools already target those pupils who, in Key Stage 2, are on the verge of a Level 4 in English. Most secondary schools are very aware of those students on the cusp between a C and D grade. This targeting of a pass grade is probably detrimental to many other pupils, high and low achievers alike. We hope that something like the existing points scoring system will become the more commonly used currency. This should mean that it is in the school's interest to raise the achievement of all, not just those near the 'pass' grade.

See the next few pages as an example of how one high school has tackled the challenge of target setting. What has been done here is equally applicable to primary schools.

How can I move ahead?

What follows is an outline of one tried and tested way of using the data which is collected in most secondary schools to set up a system of target setting.

While the focus will be on individual student target setting, the same data can be used in a different way to produce the information needed for departmental and whole-school target setting. Working with this process in schools has shown it to be well received by tutors who find it clear and easy to present to students, and well received by students themselves who like the personalised nature of what they are being offered.

The example which follows is based on the mock exam results of a group of Year 11 students. It could just as easily have been an examination within Key Stage 3 or even Key Stage 2. If target setting is to make a difference it needs to be embedded from an early stage.

Results from the mock examinations were loaded into Lotus 1-2-3 and converted into a number score (A* = 8 down to G = 1). Bar charts were created within Lotus 1-2-3 to show the results of individual students. Each bar chart contained a summary entitled 'Total points score'. A horizontal line across the chart showed the level of that student's average performance. For example a line across at the level of 4 meant that the student was scoring on average 4 points in each subject, or, in other words, was averaging a grade D.

A copy of all relevant charts was printed for the tutor and a single bar chart was given to each student. Each student had the bar chart printed in colour. That definitely seemed to make a difference to students' perception that the exercise mattered!

On the copies of the graphs given to tutors, the NFER/CATs score and a target points score had been added. These two pieces of information were not put onto the student's own chart. The target points score was derived from looking at the performance of previous cohorts of students with the same NFER/CATs score in the same school, the LEA and nationally. Targets were set towards the upper end of what previous students had achieved. It was hoped that, in this way, targets would be both fair and challenging.

Tutors proceeded to discuss the information with each student who had to, first, agree a target points score through negotiation with the tutor and, second, make a clear declaration about *where* and *how* the extra points would be produced to enable the target points score to be reached.

The exercise of comparing the students' actual points scores in the exams against their target points score was illuminating. Of course, there were a few troublesome boys who were shown to be dramatically under-achieving but there were also some very pleasant, cooperative girls and boys who were shown to be quietly getting on with under-achieving. Interestingly too, in this school, there was significant under-achievement at all levels of ability. For boys, this was mainly in the middle. It was the boys scoring an average of 90–110 in NFER tests at age 11 who were going on to under-achieve. These were the students who were moving forward to collect a list of grades D and E at GCSE, while girls with similar NFER scores were leaving with grades B and C. Looking at the performance of girls, the under-achievement seemed to be at the extremes; at the very bottom and also at the very top, where some girls seemed unable to fulfil their potential.

The first example, Figure 4.1, shows a student who is performing well, even 'over-performing', based on an NFER score of 285 gained at age 11.

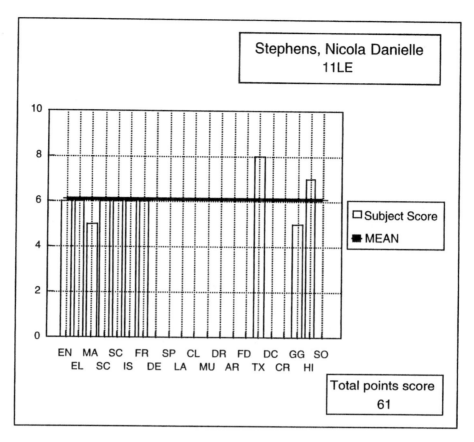

Figure 4.1

Target setting for this student becomes a positive experience of being praised, discussing the kind of learning strategies which are obviously being used to such good effect and discussing ways in which further progress can be created. The school felt the student should be aiming for 62 points in the GCSEs. In fact, following negotiation with the tutor, the student actually set the target of 'Every grade to be at least a grade B with two scores of A or A*'. In unpicking this overall target to develop precise strategies for improvement the student wrote,

> I was let down in Geography because I kept giving an example, but not explaining it. I need to collect some examples of answers that were better done than mine, and then have a go at some new examples myself. In maths I missed a page out of the booklet, probably because I was rushing. I need to practise working under timed conditions and making myself check that I have covered all the right bits.

Looking at the next two examples, Figures 4.2 and 4.3, we see a rather different story. Both students were shocked to see the gap between what they had achieved and what school thought they should be achieving. Target setting needs to start early – four months before the GCSEs is a bit late to start being shocked.

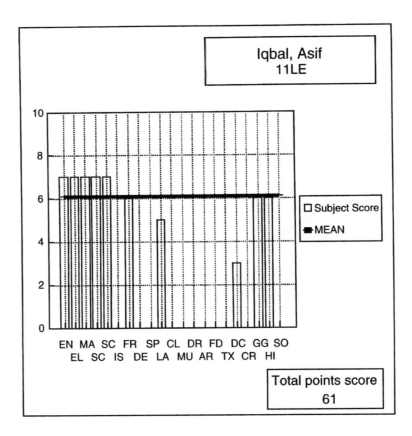

Figure: Iqbal, Asif 11LE — Subject scores (EN MA SC FR SP CL DR FD DC GG SO / EL SC IS DE LA MU AR TX CR HI), with MEAN line. Total points score 61.

Figure 4.2

The first 'under-achieving' student was seen as 'bright' – top sets all the way – but certainly not fulfilling expected potential. He had gained an NFER score of 358 at age 11.

You will notice that in the mock exams he scored exactly the same points score as the student in the previous example, and yet from a much higher level of measured potential. Through discussion with the boy's tutor, it was seen that the student needed to develop a clearer approach to note-making and keeping files organised. Homework needed to be more clearly focused and more attention needed to be given to meeting deadlines for coursework, particularly in design.

The second under-achieving student was 'a really nice lad' – he played football for the school, was always on hand to help out and was quietly getting on with failing to obtain the grades which would move him into his chosen sixth form college. He had achieved an NFER score of 300 at age 11. His mock performance showed he had only 'passed' three subjects at grade C or above, yet he needed six passes to move on to sixth form college. Failure here would mean another boy closing down his opportunities for the future. Through discussion, a target points score of 50 was agreed. English grades were lower than expected as the boy had not taken the opportunities offered to redraft coursework assignments. French had suffered through under-preparation of topics for oral assessment. In maths he had simply given up, through the sense that everyone else was moving ahead of him and he couldn't keep up. For charting a way forward, the boy devised a work schedule which would be

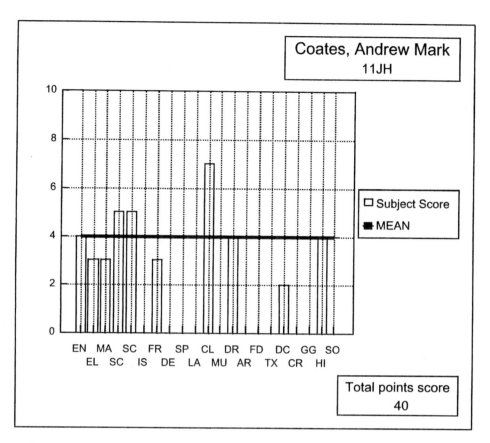

Figure 4.3

checked by his parents and best friend on a weekly basis. His best friend also agreed to work with him on a specific maths topic each week, with the emphasis on testing each other, working through past questions and preparing a twenty minute revision session for the rest of the class.

Not only were students put in charge of deciding the precise nature of their targets, and *how* these were to be achieved (no more bland statements of 'I must work harder' were allowed), but these were shared with home so that all parties knew what the 'game' was, and were regularly reviewed to see how progress was being made.

A sheet was prepared so that each of the students could attach the bar chart and declare the way forward. They were also given the fictitious performance of Gabriel Oak so that they could learn how the process worked. (See Figure 4.4.)

In Chapter 6 we look more carefully at the setting of SMART targets for individual pupils by classroom teachers. The system described above is intended to be adopted on a whole-school basis.

This bar chart shows the grades my teachers judge I am likely to achieve if I continue to work as I currently am doing. (I know that 8 points = grade A*, 7 points = grade A, 6 points = grade B, 5 points = grade C, 4 points = grade D, 3 points = grade E, 2 points = grade F, 1 point = grade G. I also know that some colleges will only count GCSE points which are scored at grade C or above.)

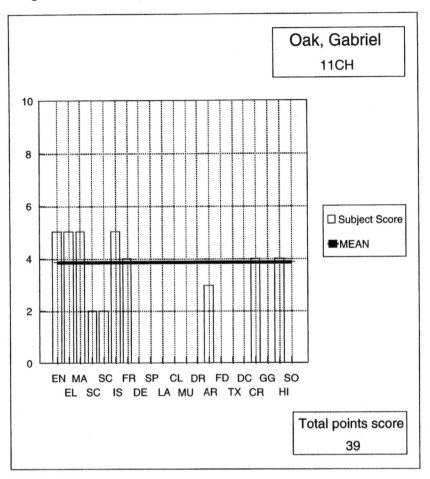

Oak, Gabriel

11CH

☐ Subject Score

■ MEAN

EN MA SC FR SP CL DR FD DC GG SO
  EL SC IS DE LA MU AR TX CR HI

Total points score

39

Having discussed my learning with my tutor, I feel that I should be aiming for .... GCSE points. I know that this points total could be achieved in various ways. I am planning to get:

.... points in .... subjects,

.... points in .... subjects,

.... points in .... subjects,

.... points in .... subjects,

.... points in .... subjects.

Figure 4.4

Looking at each of the subjects I am taking at GCSE, my targets are as follows:

Subject	Target grade	Number of points
		Total:

Looking at individual subjects, here are four **practical and precise** steps I will take to help me to move towards my targets for GCSEs.

1. ....
....
....
....

2. ....
....
....
....

3. ....
....
....
....

4. ....
....
....
....

I will share this information with my family, but I know that the responsibility for moving towards my targets lies with me.

Figure 4.4 continued

Benchmarking across good practice

The PANDAs that schools receive every Autumn term are full of statistical data that inform individual schools how they are performing both with regard to the national average and also, more interestingly, with so-called 'like schools', i.e. those schools that free school meal data suggest are likely to be similar in pupil composition. PANDAs do compare the school's gender achievement gap with the national average but not, unfortunately, with like schools. It would be very useful to identify like schools that had a much smaller gender gap, and then find out what they were doing differently. As discussed in Chapter 1, the lack of a gender gap does not necessarily mean that the school has dealt with boys' under-achievement. It may mean that both genders are happily under-achieving and nobody has noticed because there is no gap. That scenario is less likely as schools, LEAs and OFSTED will all be using prior attainment data, as discussed above.

The three essential benchmark questions should be:

- How good are we? (School's own analysis of results)
- How good can we be? (Compare own results with national averages)
- How do we get better? (Identify and visit good practice)

Schools can obtain benchmarking information by comparing themselves with schools in their own LEA. They will be able to attain data about different schools' gender gaps both as a whole, e.g. difference in 5+ A*-C at GCSE, and within subjects, e.g. difference in writing at Key Stage 1. It should then be possible to explore the background to narrower gender gaps in other schools and decide if any of their practices are transferable. Additionally, schools can use www.dfee.gov.uk/genderachievement

Literacy

Not only is English the subject in which boys show most signs of under-achievement, it is the key to further learning and helps to explain why boys under-achieve in other areas of the curriculum.

In Chapter 2, we touched upon possible reasons why boys were under-achieving so markedly in English. These included genetic disadvantage, the lack of literate role models, the changes in the curriculum and assessment methods, lack of appropriate parental support and unsympathetic classroom management. In this chapter, we want to look much more closely at some of these issues and how schools might redress the balance. Some of the methods we suggest may have been mentioned already, but in a general context. We will now focus on their relevance to English.

Raising achievement in English in the primary school

No discussion of primary school English achievement can ignore the impact of the National Literacy Strategy which most schools adopted from October 1998. For both key stages, the hour is split into four parts (see below). It is important to acknowledge that each part is also divided to some extent. For instance, the first 15 minutes should deal with what had been learned in the previous hour and what the learning objectives are for the new hour.

The literacy hour

1. Whole class – Key Stages 1 and 2 – shared text work (a balance of reading and writing) – *15 minutes.*
2. Whole class – Key Stage 1 – focused word work: Key Stage 2 – a balance over the term of focused word work and sentence work – *15 minutes.*
3. Group and independent work – Key Stage 1 – independent work while the teacher works with at least two ability groups each day on guided text work: Key Stage 2 – independent work while the teacher works with at least one ability group each day on guided text work – *20 minutes.*
4. Whole class – both key stages – reviewing, reflecting and consolidating teaching points and presenting work covered in the lesson – *10 minutes.*

The question is 'To what extent has this helped boys?' The guidance in the pack makes it clear that teaching should be:

(a) Discursive with plenty of high quality oral work. This suits boys in many ways but this may be jeopardised if teachers rely too heavily on 'hands up in class' and do not give boys the opportunity to reflect.
(b) Interactive – which again suits boys.
(c) Well-paced, 'characterised by a sense of urgency, driven by the need to make progress and succeed'. This again suits boys and reflects what we say in Chapter 6 about boys responding well to short-term challenges.
(d) Confident 'teachers having a clear understanding of the objectives', which are very well laid out in the Framework. This is fine, but teachers also need to be sure that the pupils are similarly aware of the objectives and, where possible, negotiate the objectives with pupils.
(e) Ambitious – 'creating an atmosphere of optimism about high expectations of success'. This is excellent, and could be supported by some of the suggestions made earlier regarding the school as a learning organisation, together with the celebration of success.

In short, the literacy hour, despite or perhaps because of its prescriptive nature, is a positive contribution to raising boys' achievement, but only if teachers apply their professional expertise in moulding it to the needs of their pupils and particularly to their boys. What will be the nature of the text to be discussed? The Framework sets out the types of texts to be discussed for each term but it may be a good idea to ask the pupils themselves if they have preferences for any particular text. Some teachers feel that the politically correct twenty-first century, although in many ways 'a good thing', has deprived boys of the sort of fiction they used to relish – with nothing replacing it. Maybe boys are incapable of being satisfied by the alternatives on offer. Why is there no male equivalent to the girl teen magazines of *Bliss, Sugar, More* and *Just Seventeen*? The publishers, normally so keen to exploit a market, certainly feel that boys would not be interested. There are a number of other strategies which primary schools can adopt.

1. The library

Schools should be able to consider exactly how the library could be organised to benefit boys. Boys often have less understanding than girls about how a library works. Interestingly, when they do, they can be seduced by the organisation and technology of a library and enjoy spending time in them. This means that they may be busy 'doing' things in the library but do not spend any more time reading. Giving boys responsibility within the library, of explaining its functions and organisation to younger boys, showing how the library can help them in their interests are all useful ways of raising its profile and attractiveness. This can be further enhanced if the library enjoys a wider role as the resource or information centre. Boys are attracted to ICT and the library can be made synonymous with excitement and fun, which is not the image it presently enjoys in most boys' minds.

Libraries can be used to encourage boys to read if their needs are remembered. Give it some energy, purpose and excitement! For example, a teacher could give them the task of finding some books about dinosaurs, which say three similar and three contrasting statements about them. In accepting this challenge, or an infinite number of others like it, the boys will read a great deal.

Boys and reading are not all bad news; it often depends on what has been prepared for them. Kim Reynolds from the Roehampton Institute found that 93 per cent of boys at Key Stage 2 enjoyed reading adventure stories. They preferred to read about sport, were more likely to choose a book because it was about their hobby, and selected sport, science fiction and hobbies as their preferred choice of reading matter. It is important that, having avoided certain stock for its focus on typically male stereotypes and interests, the school and its library replace it with material boys want to read, will ask to read, will be excited to read. Boys are attracted to cult/fashion reading like *Goosebumps, Animorphs* and J.K. Rowling. Boys are interested in a fantasy world (a taste later carried forward to science fiction) but one where, importantly, they can see themselves in the stories.

Boys will often respond well to 'literary lunches' in which children's authors are invited in to read their own books at lunchtime. It helps if they happen to be male, engaging and a good reader – and there is no guarantee of that. Local bookshops, the school library service and colleagues can often give advice about suitable readers.

It is interesting to ponder the mirror which boys provide for the adult world. Male authors, highly literate, tend to write from plot whereas their female equivalents tend to write from character. Perhaps we should not be surprised that boys display a different approach to literacy compared to that of girls.

The LEA's library support service will probably have ideas about the 'right kind' of stock to attract reluctant readers – which will probably be predominantly boys. Boys *do* judge a book by its cover! Choosing books with good covers, showing boys as central characters is a good idea. Some schools have asked the boys themselves to recommend reading matter – books, magazines, comics – which they think might be interesting. These are sometimes non-fictional and represent boys' interests in sport, computers and hobbies. Asking the boys themselves has the added bonus of resulting in peer group approval.

2. Partnered Reading

The idea of Partnered Reading is not new. The value of an older pupil reading with a younger one has been well recognised for some time. Prospective pupil tutors are trained with very precise instructions about exactly how to support the younger learner. In the best schemes (see end of chapter note), when and how to follow, lead and intervene are all very carefully explained – as is the importance of allowing the younger learner to choose the book and discuss its story and pictures. Partnered Reading as a concept was not developed with the under-achievement of boys particularly in mind, but some schools have made very good use of it in this context. The pairing of Year 6 boys who are themselves low or under-achievers with Year 3 boys has been very interesting. These older boys are revealed to the younger ones in roles they had not suspected. They are no longer the kickers of footballs, cock o' the school and potential or real bullies – instead they are students with skills which they are willing to share and pass on. Some schools have claimed remarkable results, but perhaps the comments of the pupils involved are just as revealing:

From the tutors:

'I couldn't read very well but I am improving as well. I'm reading more books with George (his pupil). I didn't like reading but now I do.'

(Boy, age 11)

'Sometimes when he (his pupil) has a bad day I don't enjoy it. He's made progress. When he started, I thought he had to concentrate more and now he does. He reads library books without a lot of help. It helps me too.'

(Boy, age 10)

'My partner is learning quite quickly... now he whizzes through. I think it's interesting and I like to help him.'

(Boy with behavioural problems, age 11)

'When I have been learning him I have picked up some words, and when I used to read I was very slow, but now I can read more faster. How I learned to do it I watched a video and the video told me how to do it and be a tutor.'

(Boy, age 11)

'I do my tutoring with Class 5 on their mat. I ask him to read a page and if Thomas (my partner) doesn't know a word then I break up the word or ask him to look at the picture. If there is not one and he can't read the word still I tell him the word. At the end of a page I ask Thomas to read the word he got wrong to see if he could remember the word. When there's only a minute or two left I ask him to read all the words he got wrong to make perfectly sure that he remembers the words.'

(Boy, age 11)

It is apparent that there are gains to be made through the Partnered Reading scheme that go beyond literacy. Boys find themselves in the role of carers and teachers, and the vast majority of them say that they like it. This is a wonderful opportunity to challenge the vicious cycle of boys who, denied their caring role, may go on to become outwardly uncaring partners and uninvolved parents, producing more uncaring boys. The organisation of such a scheme is harder in a secondary school because of the disruption to a complex timetable, but some schools do manage it.

The initial training of the tutors is crucial. The potential tutors love watching the training video because it gives them a chance to be critical of 'model tutors' who show them what to do, which is the intention, and to build up their own idea of good practice and self-confidence.

3. Role models

There is no greater potential than in English for the creative and effective use of role models. Primary schools can use relatives, friends and neighbours of the school to talk to the pupils, but particularly the boys, about the importance of reading and to read to them. The visiting males should have a job, a personality or an appearance which would appeal to boys – and be able to talk about reading enthusiastically. They could perhaps talk about their favourite book or the book they are reading at the moment. It does not have to be fiction. Some schools ask their visitors to bring a story to read to the children; others have a Reading Week or Fortnight when perhaps as many as twenty male visitors come into school to read.

Schools should also be aware that they have a number of visitors anyway, independent of any reading strategy. How could they be used? Can the Road Safety Officer, Police Officer, Fire Officer, Chair of Governors be asked to read? What about the caretaker or groundstaff? Some would be excellent at such a task.

Some schools use role models who can come into school to read, or listen to reading, on a regular basis. They have to be careful that these are not all older, retired people. The emphasis must be on the role model rather than their availability. The release of staff from local factories, offices and commerce is a possibility for some primary schools.

Literacy in secondary schools

The imminent national introduction of the Key Stage 3 Literacy Strategy will, hopefully, render this section largely redundant, but we feel it is still worth pursuing some strategies of a whole-school nature.

> 'As a former Head of English, I was aware that boys and girls functioned in quite different ways in regard to literacy. It wasn't simply the question of different rates of maturation, but different styles of interacting in the classroom, which, perhaps, was more obvious in the context of an English lesson than it might be in some other sort of subjects, with different traditional pedagogies in place.'
>
> (Head Teacher)

1. Working in partnership

English departments need to work in partnerships with their feeder primary schools. This may be obvious to some, but in that case why is it so often marked by its absence? The complaints from secondary schools that their students arrive semi-literate in Year 7 are legion. 'And he's got a Level 4 in his SATs!', 'He's illiterate and his teacher is innumerate', 'What's the matter with them down there?' These types of comments are not symptomatic of a united profession working together in the interests of developing the potential of the pupil. The English Department should be fully aware of the real strengths and weaknesses of their new students before they arrive. It is in English, marked out more than any other subject by its continuity and progression of skills, that true partnership has its greatest potential. When partnerships do exist it is often, quite naturally, the secondary school that leads them and administers them. It is the secondary school that is the common link, the secondary school which inherits the pupils and the secondary school which has most to gain from effective partnership.

The secondary school should ensure that its English teachers have helped the primaries to develop the concepts of the different forms in which English can be written before they change school. Colleagues in other departments can be asked to develop with their students, (*not* give them), writing frames and guidelines about how to teach them to students. These should help the newly arrived student to realise the nature of a report, an observation, an experiment, a discursive essay, and notes. It may also help to focus the assessment criteria of the different departments.

There are obviously many other activities which an active and empathetic partnership can develop. Partnered Reading and role modelling (see primary section, above) are obvious examples. Some schools have produced Theatre In Education (TIE) plays and workshops about health or bullying issues, and then toured their primary schools with it. This brings home the point that literacy is about more than reading. The subject of the TIE could be achievement or literacy or boys. Shared artists-in-residence, shared INSET, shared leaflets to parents or parents' evenings, shared book or reading weeks, shared theatre visits are other ideas. Some primary schools like their old pupils to come back to talk to their Year 6 about how English is different. The possibilities are almost endless. Just how much can be done by teachers from across the curriculum is not apparent until they sit down and talk over the issues. The onus lies with the English Department of the secondary school.

2. Role models, Partnered Reading and challenges

We have already discussed the importance of role models in the primary section of this chapter. It is just as important for the secondary student. Whether it be the staff themselves (there tend to be far more men in the secondary school) who go out of their way to portray themselves as readers via a 'What the teachers are reading this week/month' display, or having a male writer-in-residence or organising residential writers' weekends, the school should be giving the message that writing and reading are fun, cool and male activities. It may be that the nature of what is read and written becomes far wider than the set books, and this is discussed in the next section. The school should also ensure that it provides a literate environment by a variety of events and devices. Making imaginative use of notice boards is a start (can you make them interactive?). Other schools have tried suspending assemblies for a week and used all-written notices instead. Another school has a Reading Tutorial every term when the whole school (office staff included) stops what they are doing and reads silently for 20 minutes.

Partnered Reading, with help from sixth formers, might be possible to organise in some schools. It will be a telling experience for, say, a Year 8 student to be given time by the cool, car-driving, non-uniform wearing sixth former who talks to him about what he is reading and the importance of education.

Boys also like challenges. Who can find the scariest story? Who or which team can read the most books? Provide frameworks for book reviews, reading outcomes (e.g. mapping the topography of a narrative, or altering key words in an article to make the tone funny rather than scary – or vice versa) maybe in pairs or threes, and send them to the author and/or publisher. You will often get a reply. Give them team quizzes about the set texts and marry this to competition, e.g. races to the blackboard to write the correct answer to the questions given.

3. Champion the width of reading

Boys do read (albeit less than girls), but they tend to read non-fiction texts. Their comics, football, sport and hobby magazines, technical journals and Internet or Encarta information all involve the reading of English. This is not always recognised by schools, and rarely celebrated. Encouraging those boys who are interested in any kind of reading – it may not be this year's set book – to set up a display, form a small club with like-minded others (they may have done so already, but schools may be able to help), present to the rest of the class their understanding of their genre and why they like it – all these things may lead to more commitment to reading from boys. There will be many school staff whose primary reading is not the novel or a book of poetry, and it is perhaps unfair to expect boys, and girls, to reflect a different image from the one society presents to them. Diversity in reading should be expected and welcomed, but schools need to go out to find it with enthusiasm rather than simply tolerate it when it does appear.

4. Computers

We note in Chapter 6 that boys tend to like ICT and audio-visual work. The former has an image that tends to appeal to boys even if they find the reality of ICT is more about word processing than the more technical or creative potential of computers. ICT gives boys the chance to transform (downloading information, cutting and pasting, typing work up), to be social (sharing a keyboard and ideas with one or two others) and to be engaged (boys find that time flies when they are working on the computer). The computer's ability to correct spelling and grammar is, on balance, to be welcomed although teachers need to be careful that it does not result in similar effects to the indiscriminate use of calculators, which is said to have impaired the mental arithmetic of some students. The use of the new (Word 95 and later) spellchecker, which highlights misspelled words immediately, has been singled out by some teachers as a benefit as it gives instantaneous assessment and easy correction. Boys enjoy the challenge of finding information, whether it be on Encarta or the Internet, but teachers need to set tasks which expand their organisational and reading skills, e.g. find three differences between the backgrounds and influences of Wilfred Owen and Siegfried Sassoon; or download the information on Shakespeare and write a twenty line précis of his life. (Even better, do it in threes.) Not only do boys enjoy their time on the computer; it is preparing them for the future.

5. The importance of oracy

Some boys do not always enjoy reading, and they often dislike writing just as much. One secondary English Department, which enjoys the best GCSE results in a high achieving school with no significant difference between boys and girls, withdraws all pupils in small groups of 6 or 7 from its mixed ability sets once every few weeks for intensive language and vocabulary work. Nothing is written down. The Department is convinced that oral confidence and enrichment of language is the key to a more highly developed awareness and pleasure in using the written word. The key point is not the minutiae of organisation, nor the details of timetabling which enables the system to thrive, but the belief by the whole department in the merits of the system and the high expectations they engender for each other and their students.

Praise and reward system

We use the word 'system' very deliberately. One of the complaints students, but particularly boys, have about schools is the lack of consistency between different teachers' methods and generosity of rewarding. Schools need to structure and support a system which is manifestly fair and clear to use. Whether it is based on effort merits, on target-achievements, on social and community grounds or on adherence to simple tasks like punctuality and uniform, pupils and staff need to know *exactly* how it works in each class. To this end it would be advantageous if the system were designed with full participation of staff and students. If both feel that they have ownership of the system they are more likely to use and value it properly.

Some teachers have observed that boys do not like public praise, but would much prefer private praise or a letter home. If that is the situation in the school, they need to be aware of boys' sensitivities, but also be aware that such an attitude is usually the result of an anti-swot culture, which we have discussed previously.

We know that boys tend to respond well to short-term, time-limited challenges. We also know that they tend to be sociable, and like learning in social groups. A rewarding experiment in some schools has been that of group reward, based on group achievement. Whether it be punctuality, attendance (not always an advisable measure), uniform, inter-form sports, inter-form quizzes, problem-solving challenges, cycle rides or anything else which can be done collectively, some interesting developments take place. The performance of the group often depends upon the strongest helping the weakest to achieve, and the dynamics produced among the competitive boys is too complex to describe, but can quite easily be imagined. Most boys, like the girls, soon realise that the weaker 'players' will do better with encouragement and support than being shouted at – although that can help as well! It is important to design such competitions so that the same form or class does not win all the time. One way around this is to make the winner the class that shows most improvement from last time. This should encourage them all. Obviously schools could tie this form of competition in to academic achievement (reaching milestone targets or gaining effort merits) but would probably capture the support and involvement of more if they widened the activities.

The school council

The school council is very much more likely to be found in schools now than it was five years ago. This is mainly because schools rightly see it as an important contributor to the active teaching of citizenship, but also because Curriculum 2000 makes it clear that teaching should be based on pupil need. The council – be it year, key stage or whole-school – is in a very good position to ascertain boys' needs. Councils normally have representatives in all classes and they are usually capable of carrying out a survey, running focus groups when told how, organising questionnaires about any aspect of schooling. A whole-school survey on preferred learning styles would be very interesting, as would views on bullying, behaviour and discipline, rewards and general school ethos. It is important to remember, however, that there is little point in carrying out a survey unless the school genuinely intends to act on the results. Pupils become just as disillusioned with meaningless consultation as teachers.

The other purpose of a school council is to encourage boys to accept some responsibility. It is true that the very boys a school is most concerned about may be unlikely to be elected, but they can be co-opted on to working parties or on to the council itself. Feeling responsible is a major part of building self-esteem, and that is one thing many under-achievers lack.

The role of the head teacher and senior management team

The most obvious role of the senior management team (SMT) is to ensure that the strategies to raise boys' achievement are appropriate, agreed by the whole school, are written in an accessible fashion and are monitored and evaluated. This role could be better refined when thinking about the details of project management. Ideally:

(a) The head teacher is, and is seen to be, very enthusiastic in supporting the work of the school in raising boys' achievement. This means not only verbal and moral support but also finding occasional resources to fund research, planning and materials that may be necessary. The head teacher should also play an active part in the monitoring of the strategies.

(b) The head teacher or a deputy head teacher is a proactive supporter of the strategies and a regular attender at the working party or task group that the school may decide is necessary.

(c) A middle manager or aspiring younger teacher has the task of doing much of the arranging, coordinating, researching and preparation of the various whole-school initiatives of the type described in this chapter.

(d) The head teacher and SMT have to 'walk the talk' of any strategy that is agreed, e.g. if it is decided to reinforce the school as a learning organisation they should regularly be showing how they are learning – by discussion with colleagues and pupils, by display, by listening to people.

(e) As discussed in Chapter 3, the strategy should be monitored. This may mean setting milestone targets both for tasks and for their intended effects; it may mean classroom observation, depending upon what is agreed about the classroom strategies discussed in Chapter 6; it may mean discussing the whole issue with the school council on a regular basis.

(f) The SMT should be above all else good communicators. This means that they have to not only explain themselves and the school's strategies many times in different forms to different audiences – they have above all else to *listen*. They must listen to what the boys, and girls, are saying about boys' achievement. They must be fully aware of parents' and governors' views.

They should ascertain the views of the wider school community who often see otherwise unknown aspects of boys' behaviour – the school nurse, the crossing patrol lady, the cooks, lunchtime supervisors, local youth officer and more.

The role of the governing body

The governing body should be interested and concerned that the school has a gender gap in its achievement, or that any pupils are not fulfilling their potential. The governors should ask for regular reports about the head teacher's analysis of the situation and about the strategies that are being deployed to counter it. It may be appropriate to appoint a link 'gender/achievement' governor who would give moral support to the school's working party, may even serve on it, and is seen to be an important link to the local community. The whole governing body should debate the issue at least annually, and if possible attend any staff training about the issue which would both enhance their understanding and also serve as a message to the staff about how seriously it is being taken.

Note

1. See 'Shared Reading' – a video instruction pack to train pupil-tutors, available from Kirklees LEA, The Deighton Centre, Deighton Road, Huddersfield HD2 1JP Tel 01484 225793.

5 Parental involvement[1]

The best and obvious answer for parents who want to know how to help is to say that the child needs little aid other than encouragement and a place to do his work. In addition, he could be provided with bits and pieces like rulers and felt pens, and there could perhaps be one or two reference books. The latter should be treated with caution though, because parents are often too willing to buy expensive and useless books from door-to-door salesmen.

(Haigh 1975)

Pity the twenty-first century parents. Gone are the days when a satchel and dinner money were all they needed to contribute to their child's education: now they are bombarded with all manner of 'aids' to improve their offspring's academic performance, from Key Stage 1 practice SATs papers to CDs promising to enhance GCSE results.

Today, many parents see their role as much more proactive and education is no longer the right of the privileged few but an entitlement of all. With greatly increased communication opportunities, parents are able to have much more involvement in their child's school and the way in which it operates. Schools themselves are much more open and accountable, and parents are willing to play a more active role. Witness parental representation on school governing bodies, and the ease with which SATs and the dreaded performance league tables have embedded themselves into the everyday conversation of those waiting at the gate at the end of the day. This changing situation has not necessarily come about by choice but has evolved out of necessity, as the demands made on pupils to achieve increase.

Making the most of parents

Research in America (Barton and Coley 1992) has shown that parental influence in three areas – student absenteeism, varied reading materials in the home and control over the amount of television watched – can have a marked effect on student achievement. In the UK, it has been recognised for some time that parental involvement can pay long-term dividends with pupils but attempts to draw on this great, underused resource have been the

---

[1] The term 'parent' refers to anyone with primary responsibility for the pupil.

81

responsibility of the individual school rather than a comprehensive, national campaign, particularly at secondary level. If, as has been shown in Chapter 1, certain groups of boys are under-achieving and if, as mentioned above, parents are now a resource waiting to be tapped, why not make the most of them in order to raise standards?

Many of the home–school strategies described in this chapter can be effective in raising the achievement of all pupils, while others will be specific to boys. In order to gain support in raising boys' achievement, schools need to inform parents of three things:

- the existence of boys' under-achievement, the scale of the problem and the reasons behind it;
- that the school is willing to enlist parents to help to raise boys' achievement;
- what parents can actually do to help raise boys' achievement.

'Parents, we have a problem'

It is worth remembering that, whether you are trying to inform parents about the school skiing trip or about their role in raising standards, getting them across the school threshold is one matter, communicating with them efficiently and effectively is quite another. Therefore, how can a school reach out to those parents of boys who need encouragement and support?

First of all, it is important to use positive language: hitting parents with a dramatic, negative message about under-achievement will be depressing for some and a turn-off for others; rather than taking this approach, it is more constructive to focus on what boys can do and how, and where, they could improve.

Different schools find some forms of communication more effective than others; it is a question of establishing what suits the community your school serves. Also, whereas primary schools often find the personal touch more effective – talking to parents in the playground, home visits and parents coming into schools to work with their children – secondary schools, owing to their greater size, can find themselves operating on a different, more detached level and need to use more ingenious methods to promote issues and ideas.

A school should also reflect the culture of those pupils and parents it serves. Literature, notices and signs can be translated into relevant community languages and consideration can be made when planning school activities in order not to clash with religious festivals, local events, etc.

Information evenings are one way of getting a particular message across: all parents can be invited, so that no particular group feels self-conscious but, by requesting a signed reply slip, those who have not responded and whose sons are giving cause for concern at school can be identified, contacted and encouraged to participate. These evenings can be varied in format and content, and parents can be involved in interactive sessions: videos showing their children in various activities around the school or demonstrating teaching strategies can have much more impact than a monologue from the head teacher, as can group work, question and answer sessions and opportunities for parents to feed back reactions and comment.

For example, parents could be asked how they feel about the way a certain school issue was delivered to them, whether this was the best way to deal with this issue and how it could be improved. Some parents are happy to join in a whole-group discussion but others may be more comfortable filling in a questionnaire as part of the session.

Involving parents in this way means that they are far more likely to heed the advice given or carry out the tasks recommended.

'Family Fun' events (beetle drives, quizzes) for both parent and pupils, are another way of reinforcing the home/school, parent/pupil gap links, and demonstrating that learning can be enjoyable.

CASE STUDY 5.1

Lepton CE(C) J, I & N School, Kirklees LEA, near Huddersfield, has 214 pupils. The school decided to celebrate Number Day 2000 (5 December) by holding a 'Who Wants to be a Mathionnaire?' quiz show. Parents, pupils and staff went to tremendous lengths to organise this event, paying great attention to detail and Tony Caulton, Primary Inspector for Mathematics, was persuaded to act as the show's host.

All the contestants were children from the school, with eight volunteers from each year group. Mathematical questions were set at the appropriate age level and increased in difficulty as the 'prize money' rose. All contestants won a prize of some description and parents were the audience whose expertise was called upon when requested.

Head teacher, Trevor Fox, saw the event as a great success. 'It was a very enjoyable evening for everybody. It demonstrated how maths activities can be fun and brought together pupils, parents and staff in a unique way. Several parents said how much they had enjoyed themselves, despite the fact that maths had not been their favourite subject when they were at school, and others said they wished they had been able to sit in the "hot seat". I am really pleased we made the effort – the children were talking about it for some time afterwards.'

Follow up

Many parents dutifully turn up for head teacher pep talks, annual meetings, or parents' evenings and appear totally enthusiastic about school initiatives and advice given, only for the impetus to disappear shortly afterwards. If this is the case, it can be very effective if the school monitors progress of the initiative in individual families: it demonstrates the commitment of the school and can prompt parents into responding, even if only to a moderate degree.

There is also a vast army of other agencies who can assist in communicating with parents:

- educational social workers
- school nurses
- health visitors
- housing officers
- learning mentors
- LEA officers
- local librarians
- local councillors.

These colleagues can be used to reinforce the links between school and home, and to maintain the impetus for initiatives.

A parent friendly place

Teachers should bear in mind the fact that not all parents share the same enthusiasm for schools that they do. Some (a minority) may have spent the best years of their lives in such places; for others, the unchanging, heady aroma of school dinners and floor polish reminds them of long-forgotten, unpleasant scenarios from which they could not escape fast enough and to which they are now extremely reluctant to return.

For any home–school links to be effective, parents often need to be shown that schools are very different institutions from the ones they themselves attended and that the demands made on both pupils and staff have changed a great deal. This is not always initially apparent. Parents need to feel that school staff are empathetic, approachable and sensitive to the demands made on them.

The school prospectus

A parent friendly prospectus – often the first home–school link – written in everyday language and not professional terminology, can not only pave the way to understanding the school's systems and structure, but can also set the tone for the home–school partnership. It should also make clear the policy of the school on the monitoring of pupil performance and its strategies towards raising pupil achievement.

The school contact

Parents should have a designated member of staff they can contact if they have any query or cause for concern, and should be reassured that contact with the school is welcome at any time.

Parents' evenings

Parents' evenings can be a positive experience if well organised and manageable for *both* the staff and the parents. It is helpful to remember:

- the point of the evening is two-way communication and mutual understanding;
- parents need *practical* ideas to help their child, and school/departmental guidelines, written in simple terminology, can be used here (see Appendices 5.1 and 5.2 at end of chapter);
- adherence to the prescribed duration for each appointment makes everyone happier – if anything is serious enough to warrant overrunning this, you can ask parents to make an appointment to see you at another time, offer to visit them at home or call on the services of another agency to do this for you (see above);
- just as you would like to finish on time and return home to put your feet up, so would they!

Some teachers comment that the very parents they really need to see are the ones who don't turn up. Letters sent directly home rather than by pupil-mail, or by a phone call, can be used to voice your concerns; teachers can offer to see them at school or at home. Some will have genuine reasons for not attending and will welcome an alternative opportunity, while others will be convinced of the gravity of the situation by the fact that you have not let the issue slide, will be relatively receptive and will most likely attend on the next occasion. Inevitably, there will be those parents who will ignore the school's efforts. You should be philosophical about this – you cannot realistically expect to convert everybody but you can hope that the message will reach most of them eventually by natural, community osmosis.

With the growth of home access to the Internet, many schools have set up websites and post information, 'Frequently Asked Questions' and discussion issues there. Obviously, as not all homes have this facility, this will not give comprehensive coverage but it will show that the school is moving with the times, not to mention giving pupils and parents the opportunity to show off their IT skills. Parent volunteers can establish and maintain this, including those whose links with the school would be most beneficial.

The National Healthy School Standard

The NHSS was first introduced in 1999 with the aim of raising whole-school standards in environmental, psychological and physiological health, PSHCE and Equal Opportunities. It is hoped that by 2002, 50 per cent of schools nationally will be involved with the standard. Ideally, this would involve pupils, staff, parents, governors and community partners who are invited to take part in policy development, physical, social and cultural activity and to support each other's learning.

Partnerships with parents are welcomed, with facilities made available in school for their use such as designated accommodation, special notice boards, and Reading Partner schemes, and they are encouraged to become involved in policy development by means of questionnaires, parents' evenings and the PTA (Parent Teacher Association). External partners, such as the Drug Action Team or Family Planning Nurses, team up with parents to form a task group for developing healthy schools activities, and with representatives from local businesses to invite them to contribute to school life in the form of open days, help in the classroom, work placements, sponsored events and being on the governing body. Parents are also consulted about the development and implementation of home–school agreements.

The idea behind this high level of involvement is that by giving parents a sense of inclusion in, and a degree of ownership of, their child's education, they will contribute to whole-school health and create the right environment for learning, both at school itself and at home.

What parents can do to help

In order to support the school's work towards raising boys' achievement, it is vital that parents give out the right messages at home. Parents who promote a positive image towards school and learning will have a positive effect on their children's attitude. (See Appendix 5.3.)

Parents and images at home

Parents must be encouraged to read with, and listen to their child; to make time for discussion, at any age, and to give and expect reasons for ideas and opinions; to enhance/support pupils' learning topics, such as making outings to the shops with young children, or to the theatre or museums; and to display a positive attitude to school in general, i.e. attendance, coursework, and contribution to school life.

Role models

One of the reasons boys under-achieve at school is thought to be the lack of male role models. In an age when the number of single parent families is on the increase and in communities where unemployment is the norm, boys are often denied the example of a working man who contributes to the family income and ethos. At the other end of the scale, a father who works long hours or is frequently away on business (Britain has the longest working week in the EU) can have a similar effect. A boy who has a father figure/male role model, with whom he associates sharing responsibility for reading to him, supervising homework and attending parents' evenings or school functions will equate being male with being pro-school and will exemplify that himself. Help can come in the form of other trusted male members of the family or friendship circle who can help with homework, read with them, and attend school functions.

A lack of male role models in the home *can*, to some extent, be compensated by the school providing some. This may be in the form of a male teacher or another member of staff – or it may be during specially organised sessions in which males are invited in to talk about their positive experiences of education, how it has helped them, the joy of lifelong learning, how they keep on learning, etc.

Parents and the primary school

Having been the subject of nationwide government initiatives over the past few years, literacy and numeracy schemes are often a focus of schools' contact with parents. Asking parents to join in such schemes has brought interesting issues to light.

Literacy tends to generate a heartier response once parents overcome their reluctance to admit their own level of competence and accept help alongside their children, should they need it. The National Literacy Strategy (NLS) promotes the idea that showing an interest in reading and writing, in any way, is a role in itself: sharing the actual experience of reading with their children is just as commendable as encouraging them to go to the library and helping them to choose a book. It does not expect parents to act as teachers, rather as sources of enthusiasm for reading, however they are able to demonstrate this. Among many other initiatives, it supports reading partnership projects where members of the local community are trained to come into school and read with children, and parents' evenings to raise the profile of the Strategy and explain how it works and what parents can contribute (see end of chapter note).

On the other hand, while parents are less self-conscious about their standard of numeracy, some are still haunted by their own unhappy experiences in mathematics and pass on this fear or dislike of the subject to their children. Acknowledgement of this problem is made by the National Numeracy Strategy (NNS) which not only encourages teachers to make mathematics enjoyable and success achievable, but (in some LEAs) reaches out to parents to encourage them to treat the subject positively with their children and not to let the 'I hate maths' syndrome remain a vicious circle.

The Basic Skills Agency also plays a major role in the attempt to raise standards in these two subjects, with Element Nine of its Primary Quality Mark (PQM) requirements focusing entirely on parental involvement. It requires that the school informs parents about opportunities for involvement, support and improvement of basic skills in their children's school and of the progress of under-attaining pupils at least three times in an academic year. Its Case Study guide for this element shows how successful PQM schools have made use of:

- Family Literacy/Numeracy sessions, where parents of targeted children can help at whatever level suits them;
- Family Learning Support – linking with local colleges to support parents who lack confidence in their own literacy/numeracy skills;
- Dads 'n Lads groups, where there is particular concern about boys' under-achievement and to emphasise male role models.

CASE STUDY 5.2

Beech EY, I & J School, Huddersfield (Kirklees LEA) has 187 pupils on role. It has just been awarded the Basic Skills Agency Primary Quality Mark. Head teacher, Tina Warden, describes how the school has achieved the parental involvement element of the award.

Initially, some of our parents were not overtly interested in becoming involved with their children's learning and were reluctant to even come to the school itself.

We encouraged them to attend courses as part of the 'Helpers in School' project and 'Living and Working with Under 8s', for which we were funded by the Single Regeneration Budget. One graduate of the course has gone on to become a CSA (Classroom Support Assistant), a staff governor and is now involved in the study support programme 'Yorkshire Arts and Music'.

Friday mornings are coffee mornings and parents are encouraged to attend with their younger children. We have also run the 'Babies into Books' scheme and 'Reading Friends' where local people, mainly senior citizens, work with a small group of children helping them to interrogate text.

Another initiative we support is the 'Share Project', where parents come into school on a weekly basis and are given tasks to work on with their children at home. Originally, we intended to offer this to Year 1 pupils and then extend it to Year 3.

The important point to remember is not to expect one grand strategy to solve everything: different parents react to initiatives in different ways and not all ideas will be a success across the board. For instance, the Share Project got a good initial response from parents but has not received the same support this year, so we are having to rethink. You have to get to know your parents really well – we have two members of staff with a specific remit to strengthen parental relations – and approach them in a number of different ways with the hope that one or some of them will work.

The best method of communication is definitely one-to-one: it generates mutual respect and helps to dispel the anti-school culture which can be so damaging.

Of course, involvement in such activities depends on parental willingness and opportunity to contribute their time. In some communities, it would be unheard of for both parents to take on such a role, especially fathers. In others, particularly those with high levels of unemployment, it can provide the perfect opportunity to benefit the child and parent simultaneously. Nor, as before, does support have to be limited to immediate family members: aunts and uncles, or grandparents are often willing to play their part – any suitable person can be recruited in the cause.

Parents and the secondary school

Parental involvement in the secondary school raises new issues. Parents may have come to terms with providing support in literacy and numeracy but, all of a sudden, they feel they are required to be an expert in ten subjects across the curriculum! It is easy for them to feel out of touch or rejected. How can the school maintain the momentum of their previous involvement, and encourage those who have yet to make an input?

Guidelines from each department setting out ways in which parents can support their child's work in particular subjects would be useful. Ways in which parents can help with homework could also be circulated. It would be helpful if this was done as part of a whole-school plan as parents could find themselves being asked to support more subjects than is feasible in a particular timescale. Support can mean a myriad of things:

- testing vocabulary, facts and methods;
- helping with research in the local library or on the Internet;
- finding TV programmes, films, videos, local theatrical productions, or sporting events to support set texts or projects. (See Appendix 5.2 at end of chapter.)

Parents as drug educators

One topic that often interests boys as much as their parents is that of drug education. Many locally produced drug education programmes supply drugs awareness evenings for parents, but the best of them go further. 'Parents as Educators' from Kirklees LEA is one example of a programme that is designed to help parents talk to their children, especially their sons, about drugs. Typically, parents and children attend an evening meeting, during the first hour of which the pupils take part in a series of learning activities with teachers or other volunteers and the parents get a quick introductory session identifying types of drugs and the effects they can have. In the second half, after coffee/tea/juice, children rejoin their parents to undertake some joint exercises about drugs. The parents have in effect become the educators.

It is a powerful learning experience for boys to hear their parent(s) discussing such ideas and opinions with others, and parents recognise the fact that the school is delivering something positive, relevant and worthwhile.

Parent/Teacher Associations

Parent Teacher Associations/Friends of School are an excellent way of involving parents in school life but need promoting as so much more than selling raffle tickets and baking buns – so as to set a good example to boys, reinforce links between school and home, give parents a sense of contributing to school life and provide vital support to the teaching staff.

Parents who wish to take their involvement a step further can also stand for the governing body where they can play a direct role in the running of the school. While individuals are required to undergo a ballot process to serve as a parent governor, it can prove a profitable exercise for parents of targeted, under-achieving pupils to be encouraged to stand for election, thus making them an integral part of the very machinery of the school. With this responsibility, it is likely that parents will pay more attention to their own child's behaviour, attitude and performance.

And finally...

Parents need to feel included and welcome in their child's school and to receive achievable, realistic ideas to put into practice at home. It is vital that they work in conjunction with the school and not antagonistically, and as they may not be familiar with current educational ideas and techniques, they need support from those who are. Home is not an extension of school – school is ordered and patterned, while home is freestyle and more expressive – this means that different rules apply and different expectations can be made.

The contribution that parents make can be invaluable; schools can neither demand nor depend on this contribution but should use it to complement their role. In their efforts to raise achievement, schools should see parents as a powerful ally.

> Without parents and the wider community on board, the humane school environment that is comfortable with diversity, that is truly socially inclusive and supports achievement and the striving for it, can't hope to survive outside its four walls. Parents not schools exert the strongest influence on children.
>
> (Klein 2000a)

Note

1. See 'Paired Reading' – a video for parents which explains very clearly *how* parents can listen to their children read in a developmental and supportive way. Available from Kirkless LEA, The Deighton Centre, Deighton Road, Huddersfield HD2 1JP Tel 01484 225793.

APPENDIX 5.1

Primary Pro-forma

Autumn Term – Focus _____

Dear Parent/Carer

Thank you for your interest in your child's learning. Below are some ideas for activities you could share with your child this term. We are not suggesting that you do *all* of these but any you can manage. We hope you enjoy doing them together.

1. Listen to your child read.

2. Read to your child.

3. Alternate the above, by page or by paragraph.

4. Go on an information hunt linked to a current topic on children's TV, in newspapers, at a local museum, on the Internet.

5. Go *with* your child to your local library; help them choose books, both fiction and non-fiction, linked to the topic chosen for 4 above, or a subject of interest.

6. Help your child keep a diary.

7. Start writing a story with your child, linked with the above topic. Add three new sentences a day or more if 'in the mood' and you have time.

8. Go through 'Times Tables' with your child but do it in a situation your child will find relaxing, e.g. while on a walk, in the car, in a comfy chair together, etc.

Note
It is important that you and your child read different types of literature – fiction, poetry, newspaper articles about their favourite football team, menus in a burger bar – whatever you can lay your hands on to give them variety.

APPENDIX 5.2

Secondary Pro-forma

Humanities Department – History
Year 10
The Wall Street Crash

Dear Parent/Carer

Thank you for your interest in your son's/daughter's learning. If you could provide support in any of the following ways, it could prove beneficial to his/her progress.

It will help your son/daughter to make notes when he/she finds any relevant information.

Task	Date completed
Test on Fact Sheet 1.	
Help pupil to look for any articles related to The Wall Street Crash:	
in newspapers/magazines	
in your local library	
on the Internet	
on television	
on video ('The Grapes of Wrath' – shows consequences of Crash).	
Act out attached two-part play on Crash, swopping roles.	

APPENDIX 5.3

Tips for Parents of Boys
(for school to give to parents)

1. Don't do too much for them – e.g. at age five they should be tying their own shoelaces, dressing themselves, helping with chores around the house such as washing up, tidying their bedroom, and generally learning responsibility.

2. Teach them to be organised: homework should be done as soon as possible, not after TV, etc.; school bags should be packed before bedtime rather than in a rush in the morning.

3. Give them short-term rewards rather than long-term ones.

4. Help them to meet male mentors – cousins, uncles, friends, etc.

5. Try to encourage a culture of 'caring masculinity' – e.g. boys do babysitting, help care for older relatives, and are not afraid to discuss feelings. Don't say 'Big boys don't cry' but help them to show a non-macho side of their personality.

APPENDIX 5.4

Possible Questions for Parents' Evenings (*The Kirklees Parent,* March/April 2001)

1. What, exactly, is my child learning and at what level?
2. How is the school teaching that?
3. What can I do at home to help?
4. What is my child good at?
5. Is there anything my child is particularly good at?
6. What is my child finding hard? How can I help?
7. Does my child try hard enough?
8. What can I do to help my child try harder?
9. Does my child join in class discussions?
10. How can I help with my child's school work overall?
11. Is my child happy at school?
12. Has my child made friends?
13. Are you worried about my child's behaviour?
14. Can I see some of my child's work?

6 Classroom management to raise achievement

Introduction

In this chapter, we consider a menu of strategies that year groups, departments or individual teachers could use to help raise achievement: they are the *micro strategies* mentioned in Chapter 3. They are not normally whole-school strategies, although there is no reason why every teacher in the school could not adopt them, but have been discussed and adopted by the subject departments (in secondary schools) or by year or key phase groups in primary schools. There is no reason why individual teachers should not adopt individual strategies, but our experience suggests that these strategies can be undermined if other colleagues, teaching similar pupils in the same subject/key phase, do not give support.

The teacher as reflective practitioner

We do not expect all the strategies to work. There is no magical blueprint for raising boys' achievement and some strategies may be inappropriate for some teachers. Their personality, ingrained teaching style, subject or reputation may make it difficult for them. We want teachers to regain the confidence to try things out, to fail, make mistakes and learn. It is a prerequisite of a learning organisation, as explored in Chapter 4, that failure is accepted as an inevitable facet of learning. It may not be the perceived culture of our target setting times but honest failure is healthy and necessary if long-term success is to be achieved.

Expectation

If teachers expect boys to under-achieve, then some of them probably will; the same could be said of pupils from minority ethnic groups or deprived backgrounds. Teachers know this; they can wax lyrical about the importance of expectations at interviews; they are intellectually committed to having high expectations for all, but the negation of the concept is all too evident in the everyday experience of education. The head teacher who says that his .SATs will suffer this year because of a preponderance of boys in the cohort, the class teacher who winces when she finds that the two new pupils are from 'the estate', the LEAs which set much lower targets for pupils from minority ethnic backgrounds – all are lowering their expectations of their pupils. There may be a professional discussion to be had here about reality and aspiration, but teachers should try to be honest with themselves. If they are internalising low expectations, do they really expect to keep that hidden? Do they think that the normal betrayers – body language, facial expression, vocabulary and nuance – can be denied? It may, at times, be appropriate to discuss the importance of expectation with the class and individual pupils. In secondary schools, this could be taken to a very sophisticated level.

Classroom teachers have the opportunity of giving and getting high expectations for boys. The language used is important. 'Boys are learners', 'you will succeed', 'failure is not an option' set the tone. When reprimanding boys for behavioural or achievement lapses, high expectation can be maintained. 'This is so unlike you', 'you're capable of far better', 'not the effort a boy like you puts in' helps the pupil to define, or redefine, himself as a high achiever. At the same time, it is critical that negative comments are avoided: 'Typical!', 'Why can't you be like your sister/the girls/somebody else', 'I expected nothing better' will undermine all the good work.

The start of a lesson can also be critical for setting high expectations. It is a good idea to start with success. Ask questions that you *know* will be answered correctly. Give praise and make positive asides about the ability in the classroom – 'this is the best class in the year/school', 'the boys in this class are so talented/hard working'. It is also possible to set high expectations by discussing the learning objectives for the lesson. 'By the end of the lesson you will have learned x and y; it won't be easy but I think you can do it.' The discussion about achieving very specific learning outcomes is particularly beneficial to many boys who are motivated by short-term challenges and goals.

Brain gym/warm-ups

In the 1980s, teachers were encouraged to have warm-up sessions with their classes. These were normally physical, contrived movements in which the purpose was either to energise the class or, and especially after lunchtime, to cool them down and prepare them for more reflective work. There was not a great deal of theory behind it, mainly an intention to get the class in the right mood to work, but it worked quite well for many teachers.

A more scientific approach is now available. As we know more about the brain (see next section), we also know that it is desirable that boys try to work with both hemispheres – a feat that often eludes them. There are number of 'brain gym' books available that give exercises to help this to happen (allegedly!). These may include things like alphabet semaphore (see Appendix 6.1 at end of chapter) and old favourites like rubbing the head with one hand while patting the stomach with the other. It is the physicality of such coordinated activity that helps to engage both the hemispheres.

Boys' learning styles

A great deal of research has taken place over the last ten years about the issue of how boys and girls tend to differ in their preferred learning styles, and much of this has focused on the growing understanding of how the brain works. We do not intend to rehearse all those arguments now, rather to give a synopsis of the main findings and their relevance to the classroom. We are very anxious to emphasise the fact that gender does not predetermine the favoured learning styles of boys or girls. One can only point to a *tendency* for boys to favour certain styles, while acknowledging full well that hundreds of thousands of them do not fit comfortably into the stereotype. Likewise, many girls much prefer a different style of learning from that ascribed to them by brain research.

Male and female brains

Male	Female
■ Tend to use right brain more than the left – *can reproduce a pattern by walking it out on the floor, solve problems requiring mathematical reasoning.*	■ Hemispheres tend to be more integrated which helps with problem solving and multi-tasking.
■ Tend to use only one hemisphere at any one time – tend to be focused and dogmatic.	■ Better connections between hemispheres – girls have language parts in each hemisphere.
■ Tend to be better at three dimensional work *building with bricks, solving puzzles.*	■ Larger area for linguistic processing – talk, read and write earlier than males, out perform boys at all key stages.
Much of our understanding of this has come from the work of Geoff Hannon (1997) and Trevor Hawes (1998).	

Figure 6.1 Male and female brains

Learning preferences – visual

- 29 per cent of people learn best by storing a series of images in their brain.
- They learn best when able to use pictures, mind maps, diagrams, flow charts, visual artefacts, key words display, colour, TV, video camera, ICT, posters.

Learning preferences – auditory

One in three (34 per cent) of people learn best through sound. Typically, they would like:

- paired and grouped discussion;
- tapes, debates, rhyme, repetition, lecture, dramatic readings;
- music;
- teacher explanation;
- ICT.

Learning preferences – kinaesthetic

Likewise, about one in three (37 per cent) of people learn best through movement or touch. Typically they would like:

- ICT;
- experiments;
- field trips;
- sequencing and ranking cards;
- placing events on a timeline;
- physical movement – role play, break-states, brain gym.

Male and female learning styles

In considering Figure 6.2 it should be remembered that as with many other aspects of gender there is huge variation within the same gender as well as between them.

Learning styles

- Visual – we remember images, shapes and colour.
- Auditory – we remember voices, sounds and music.
- Kinaesthetic – we remember by doing, moving and by touching.

Male	Female
■ Higher level of testosterone – more concerned with competing than cooperating – *will interrupt in class – are competitive.*	■ Lower level of testosterone – in general quieter and more compliant.
■ Lower level of serotonin – leads to greater risk taking, behavioural problems – *will experiment, good at problem solving.*	■ Higher level of serotonin – able to analyse data more rationally and thus control behaviour through greater understanding of emotions.
■ Lower level of dopamine – greater level of stimulation needed – *short attention span.*	■ Higher level of dopamine – lower need for stimulus, hear better and listen longer and more effectively.

Much of our understanding of this has come from the work of Geoff Hannon (1997) and Trevor Hawes (1998).

Figure 6.2 Male and female learning styles

Arguably, our other two senses, taste and smell, could also influence our preferred learning style – but there is far less scope for employing these within teaching and learning. The relevance of this to boys' achievement is that more boys than girls favour a kinaesthetic style – but English schools tend to put heavy stress on the other two styles. Many pupils prefer to learn in one or two of these ways – rarely all three. It may well be that some under-performing boys would do much better if they were given a richer, kinaesthetic learning diet.

Gardner's Multiple Intelligences

Howard Gardner has suggested that there are eight different sorts of intelligence (see Figure 6.3), although far from all of them have been recognised in educational practice.

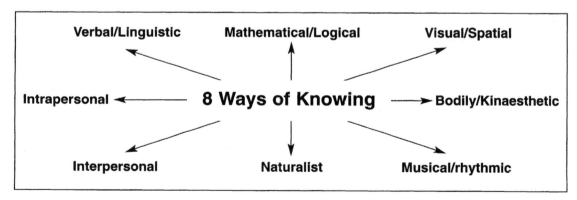

Figure 6.3 Gardner's Multiple Intelligences

Traditionally, the visual/spatial and mathematical/logical have tended to predominate in schools, and were the basis of the IQ tests that were sometimes used to determine ability. In Figure 6.4 we have tried to link the Intelligences to different learning styles.

Learning styles	Multiple Intelligences
• Visual	☐ Visual–Spatial
	☐ Logical–Mathematical
	☐ Intrapersonal
	☐ Naturalist
• Auditory	☐ Linguistic
	☐ Mathematical–Logical
	☐ Interpersonal
	☐ Intrapersonal
	☐ Naturalist
• Kinaesthetic	☐ Bodily–Kinaesthetic
	☐ Visual–Spatial
	☐ Musical Rhythmic
	☐ Naturalist

Figure 6.4 Intelligences and learning styles

Characteristics of pupils with a kinaesthetic learning preference

Much of our understanding in the area has been informed by the work of Trevor Hawes and Geoff Hannon. Pupils with a kinaesthetic learning preference:

- are active and athletic;
- learn best when *doing* what is being taught;
- like variety;
- make things;
- think best when moving;
- need to move in the classroom and to touch objects;
- fidget and move their legs;
- beat out rhythms on desks;
- play with any object within reach;
- stand at the teacher's side asking questions.

Kinaesthetic learning style and the impact on boys' progress

If boys form a preponderance of kinaesthetic learners and there is a dearth of kinaesthetic learning techniques being employed by the school, it is likely that some boys will fall into a vicious circle of under-achievement confirmed by failure and disillusionment.

Some boys arrive in Year 8 believing that they are stupid, slow, badly behaved, disruptive, that they will not improve as learners and that learning is a negative experience. The challenge is to help these boys to improve their learning skills and their self-esteem.

Strategies for the kinaesthetic learner

- Cutting/pasting sequence of notes.
- Doing experiments.
- Doing hands-on or tactile activities.
- Having something to squeeze or hold.
- Miming.
- Moving book from side to side while reading.
- Moving to different places for different tasks.
- Moving while learning, i.e. stepping, clapping.
- Using ICT.

Resources

- Anything physical or movable, dance, field trips, hands-on experiences.

Memory techniques for the kinaesthetic learner

- Connect ideas to physical movements.
- Change positions while listening/learning different ideas.
- Follow words with finger when reading.
- Keyboarding.
- Shuffling key word cards.
- Writing in air or on arm, leg, or somebody's back.

Some suggested kinaesthetic practices in the classroom

Some of the ideas below were suggested at a NASEN conference in Belfast in 2000.

In their seats

- ICT.
- Spell out an answer using an elbow, in the air.
- Brain gym – trace out 'Lazy Eights' on their desk top or in the air.
- 5/4/3/2/1 – each of the pupils point to 5 blue items/4 pictures of kings/3 rectangular objects/2 opposite words/1 hand made object.

- All subjects – which character in the book/play/situation am I? – without talking, on mannerisms alone.
- Take five deep breaths to centre and focus or practise methods for self-control (temper/breathing/focus, etc).
- Short break state – for five seconds, look at ceiling, then front left corner of room, then desk top, then front right corner of room.
- Putting cards/Post-its in order on the desk top, i.e. to make a sentence, to place events in chronological order, to show cause/effect (all subjects).
- When reviewing a topic, distribute cue/key word cards among the more kinaesthetic pupils which they can hold up as the point is reached/discussed.
- When learning/reviewing a topic, use mind mapping, create a logo, draw.
- To celebrate a success, e.g. completing a project, finishing a topic, give the pupil to your right and left a 'High Five'.
- Have the pupils stand up at their desks and answer questions in their alphabetical name/birthday month order.
- Two pupils change seats.

On one spot

- Maths – buying goods in a shop and getting the correct change.
- Languages – playing out life scenes.
- Standing at the desk, stretch each arm and then both as high as possible towards the ceiling in order to increase oxygen levels in the body.
- As they stand at the end of the class, cup all the knowledge they came into the classroom with in their left hand and then cup all the knowledge they have learnt in that particular lesson in their right hand. Everyone places their right hand over their left hand and quietly together says 'Yes'.
- Circle Time – if a controversial subject is to be discussed, keep passing a 'conch shell' to ensure that as many pupils as possible can speak.
- 'Everybody stand up please. I'd like you to sit down when I come to the time you went to bed last night' (start calling out the time in 15-minute intervals from 8 o'clock onwards until everyone has sat down).
- Tiptoeing on the spot.

Moving around the classroom

- Acting out improvised scenes, e.g. drugs scene, sexual harassment. English/Drama – actual scenes from plays or books.
- One pupil during each class can pin an icon from the edge of the student board onto its centre or onto the blackboard, from a predesigned selection.
- Putting cards/Post-its in order on the floor, i.e. to make a sentence, to place events in chronological order, to show cause/effect (all subjects).
- Pupils holding key word cards are placed around the room. As the topics referred to on their cards are prioritised, put in categories or placed in size or chronological order, the relevant pupils form a queue.
- Treasure hunts for the answers to problems, i.e. from the walls, on display areas, stuck below desks.

The boy friendly classroom

Educational practice should become friendlier to boys' learning styles by adopting some of the practices listed below.

- Allow controlled movement – tell the class why this will help them to learn – brain gym, break states.
- Allow boys to hold and squeeze a small piece of sponge or rubber ball.
- Learn by 'trying out' rather than being told about – investigative learning such as experiments in science, or practical maths.
- Trace out words on a partner's back.
- Use practical maths – allow finger multiplication.
- Build on boys' spatial awareness – give them success with plans and maps – teach them to use mind maps.
- Teach boys to set and meet targets.
- Build up a collection of objects for pupils to touch.
- Encourage target-directed motor skills – success in football, rugby, cricket, outside the classroom will improve self-esteem in the classroom by using success rehearsal.
- Make use of word processing for as many writing tasks as possible.
- Help boys to organise their work – structure their writing, use diagrams, writing frames. (Note: writing frames work best when they are designed by the class with the teacher, not just given to the class, as all pupils can then understand the purpose and have some ownership.)
- Act out stories and events – written tasks can be TV script, a newspaper's report on an event.
- Allow for competition – hold quizzes such as Who Wants To Be A Mathionnaire as described in Chapter 5.
- Use ICT as part of teaching and learning.
- Put images of successful role models for boys on the walls – buy into their world!
- Put the learning in context – why are we learning this? Show the 'Big Picture' of the complete jigsaw before working on one of the parts. It helps to give direction and purpose.
- Break the learning into chunks and tell pupils how long each task will be.
- Appeal to boys' competitive and risk-taking streak. Try problem-solving challenges in a limited but *feasible* timespan. Boys like to know that they *can* win.
- Use mind maps to brainstorm, to plan writing or to summarise a topic.

Target setting

Setting SMART targets

The really significant work in individual target setting is not the production of coloured graphs, impressive and motivating as they are: it is the negotiating and agreement of targets with the students. It is very easy to do this badly. The two principles that should guide you are that the individual student must feel that they are *genuinely* his or her targets, not imposed by a harassed class teacher who gives off messages that he or she would really prefer to do something else. This means that sufficient planning, time and training have to be given to it by the school. The second principle is that the targets should be SMART, not sloppy or soft, see below and Figure 6.5.

SMART target setting

SMART targets are Specific, Measurable, Achievable, Realistic, Time-limited.

Note the change of verb in the SMART target column of Figure 6.5. 'Will' suggests less coercion and more certainty than 'must'. A variation on this theme is to use a form of neuro-linguistic programming to create more visionary targets. Thus the first SMART target could be changed to 'I'm pleased that I'm taking six spellings home every week, and getting Tom to test me on Tuesdays and Thursdays for the next two weeks'. The verb has

Sloppy target	Soft target	SMART target
I must improve my English	I must improve my spelling	I will learn six spellings each week and get Jane/Tom/Dad to test me on them at home on Tuesday and Thursday for the next two weeks.
I must be better behaved	I must improve my behaviour in history and French	I will sit apart from Andy in French and Gaz in history. I will not talk when the teacher is talking. I will get off yellow report by the end of term.
I must do better in science	I must improve my practical work in science	I will plan carefully five steps for each practical. I will ask questions if I'm unsure what to do next. I will put away the apparatus at the end of the session.

Figure 6.5 SMART targets

changed to the present, and the sentence has been injected with emotion. You should be aware that the emotion has to *genuinely* come from the pupil, (risible laughter from the sceptics), but they may be surprised. Many pupils welcome the chance to find a way, *their own way*, forward in their work (Tice 1997). The timespan, two weeks, has been kept deliberately short to suit boys' preferences. It can always be reviewed and extended for another two weeks if necessary. Teachers are the best judges of the optimum timespan for individual boys. The first target is also social – it holds out the reward of the sort of social contact boys seem to enjoy in their learning.

Obviously, most students will need help to find appropriate strategies and Appendix 6.2 has a number of suggestions that can be adapted and used as a starting point.

Seating policy and learning zones

A habit has grown in many British schools of allowing students to sit in self-selected seats. It is in the traditions of a liberal, empowering society that this should be so. Unless you interfere with others why should you not sit where you want? It is a sloppy habit, though, if held up to examination. If children are in school to learn should we not do all we can to assist the process, even if it means going against their initial wishes? After all, we impose uniform, school rules and assemblies on children. Why do we think that a seating policy, which is central to their learning, should be different? A pupil in a classroom occupies what we have come to call a 'learning zone'. This zone is fairly flexible. Most of the time it consists of the desk of the learner, plus the desks and personalities of the other one, two or three pupils in the same block, or pair. Occasionally the zone will change shape completely as the teacher engages the individual or the whole class. The zone could take the shape of a corridor of learning or widen out during whole-class discussion to be a hall of learning but its most enduring features will be dominated by the shape and character of the learners in the immediate vicinity. If pupils have a free rein about choosing their friends as neighbours, they will invariably choose those who share the same values. Thus an under-achieving boy will choose to sit next to another under-achieving boy, and the same with the girls. These will naturally support each other's lack of effort, initiate each other into the anti-swot club and be unchallenged by any competing values – save that of the teacher. The classroom will soon become pockmarked with burgeoning ghettos of under-achievement. Schools should thus regard the learning zone of individual pupils as a manifestation of the learning school. The classroom is principally the place to learn.

The teacher must carefully consider which learning styles would be complementary. She or he may put a verbally confident but under-achieving boy with one who is reflective and would benefit from some of the confidence his new partner has; another under-achiever who is a poor presenter of work with a girl who is excellent at this; a girl who in under-achieving in mathematics with one who has the skill and patience to help her through it. All have been placed for reasons of learning, not of behaviour, and that is a vital distinction to make when introducing it to the class. They will be much more willing to accept the former rather than the latter. This seating pattern is not fixed. One head teacher has suggested that 'students should be entirely comfortable in working with everybody else in the room'. It is an ambitious but achievable goal. It would necessitate the regular, perhaps half-termly, change in seating positions but, as one head of English who has used such a system stated 'It means there are no cosy corners where people are just coasting'.

Teachers will make mistakes in seating plans, although less frequently with experience. It will soon become an accepted norm in the school and is ideally started at the beginning of the academic year, although some schools have introduced it as late as Christmas in Year 11.

> 'Initially it did cause some questions, but it soon became fine. In the past I sometimes felt that you have one table which was drawing my attention – and it was often a male-dominated table – whereas now my attention is around the whole class.'
>
> (Head of Art, Northern Comprehensive)

So much depends on the way it is introduced and adhering to the rigid rule that you are primarily concerned with learning. This helps to emphasise the image of the school as a learning organisation. Some teachers have announced to the class at the beginning of the year that by the end of it they will have worked intensively with every other student in the room. In other words, seating positions are regularly being shifted. The result of this has generally been beneficial. It has cut down the amount of teasing, taunting, name-calling, poking and bullying as for the first time the pupils get to know *all* their classmates – or anticipate having to work with them. For youngsters growing up in multicultural, pluralistic Britain, the more they have to work with different sorts of people, the better for all concerned.

The system is not a panacea. Some teachers, surveying their hard-working, well behaved girls, quite rightly want to protect them and their work from a bunch of wild boys who they just cannot see would be influenced for the better. Raising the achievement of boys should never be done at the expense of the girls, as we have been at pains to make clear, but girls are under-achieving as well, sometimes in different ways from the boys. We would argue that the glass ceiling will continue until girls get more used to taking risks, speculating and causing upsets. The present National Curriculum, with its rewards for patient hard work may not do a great deal of favours to girls in the longer run.

The teacher may decide to place the desks together in groups of four, a common strategy in primary schools. The advantage of this is that it gives more scope for planning a stronger influence upon the under-achiever. She or he may now have three achievers exuding good practice. The disadvantage is that – if the numbers don't work out – you can be left with two under-achievers on the same table again. There is nothing wrong 'per se' with this. It all depends where the balance of influence lies and is a decision that has to be the product of professional reflection.

Teachers should be aware that seating plans in the manner described can be controversial, which is one of the reasons it is so important to have an effective awareness-raising strategy. Parents do not always like the idea of choice being taken from their children, nor that their little Marie-Louise is forced to sit next to Sam-Who-Keeps-Ferrets. Never mind that Sam is terrified of her. An important aspect of any seating policy is that it is flexible. It can be changed if things do not work out. The pupils know that, they know why they've been asked to sit in a certain place and they know their role there – whether it be to learn from, or to show and encourage, another. The teacher, it is accepted, is in charge of managing learning in the classroom.

Group work

By group work we mean learning when the pupils have to work together, not when they are sitting together but engaged in individual work. Boys, we have discussed earlier, tend to prefer being social learners, and group work will help them. Group work also helps to optimise the effects of having a planned seating policy. Under-achieving boys who have been placed in groups for specific reasons – of which they are aware – may well find that the very aspects of learning where they are weakest are regularly exemplified for them. The sort of things where group work is at its best are:

- problem-solving, particularly something concrete like tower-building;
- group opinion on a controversial subject, such as capital punishment or school uniform;
- conducting an experiment or survey where group members have different tasks which build to a coherent whole;
- production of a multifaceted piece of work, such as a newspaper or a display;
- a quiz or challenge based on teams.

It can be interesting to ask individuals their opinion, of each other as learners, or of an issue, both before the group work and again afterwards. Teachers may well build into lesson objectives that the pupils come to realise the function, benefit and potential of group work. As when thinking about a seating plan, the teacher needs to be careful about the composition of the group and also that the task is appropriate to group work. In one school, the teacher wrote comments on the board about the quality of the group work going on. 'Group A working well together', 'Group B listening well to each other', 'Group C making good use of resources' – all reinforced the fact that cooperative working was one of the learning objectives and also gave positive messages to all the groups. The students really enjoyed and responded to this immediate feedback. At the end of the lesson, the teacher gave them a score on the quality of their group work. Thus the process of learning, as well as the outcomes, are being valued in the eyes of the students.

Some teachers have reported that boys prefer working in pairs rather than groups. This is fine if they are in productive, achieving pairs but care needs to be taken to ensure that the pairs are more than a social or comfort zone: they have to be learning zones as well. Pairs can be a precursor to a group of four, with the comfort zone provided of working with another of the same gender.

Marking

Feedback and marking play an important part in raising the interest in success of all students. Unfortunately, it has often played the role of confirming students' more negative suspicions about their abilities. This is particularly true of boys who may find that their areas of weakness – tidiness and presentation – are commented upon, even scorned, by teachers. Tell anybody enough times that they are untidy, or sloppy, or lazy and they will soon feel obliged to live up, or down, to this image. The general rule should be that pupils need to be moved forward from where they are, not bogged down in repeated failure. Hence, when marking teachers should:

1. Be very clear when the work is set about *exactly* what they will be looking for. It is an unwise teacher who tries to mark all aspects of every piece of work – that way madness lies. It may be an idea to ask the students to write on top of their work the aspect that is being marked. *Never* have more than three aspects or 'things' which are being marked.
2. Try to avoid commenting on presentation unless really necessary.
3. Try to give more positive comments than negative ones. This does not mean that mistakes or poor work should be ignored, but feedback is an opportunity to ask the students to question the whole relationship they have with their work and, if necessary, to challenge the image they have of themselves as learners. If a mistake is pointed out, it should be made clear why it is wrong. If it is a first or unusual mistake in this aspect of the work, make it clear that it is unlike the student to make it. If it *is* typical of the individual, then emphasise that he or she is too good to make such errors. In other words, the teacher is building an image in the students' minds of them as successful learners. A specific idea for improving work is also much more useful than 'try harder' (e.g. count the number of sentences; count the number of full stops; is either 'winning'? It should be a draw).
4. Consider the use of peer assessment. Not only does it give boys time to reflect on their work, and that of others, it should lead to a discussion about what exactly good work is and what gains high marks.
5. Show the class a previously completed example of good work. Photocopy it. Homework could be to find five good things about it.
6. Consider using another sort of pen. Some teachers are very keen that red pen is not used, and suggest that a green pen is far less aggressive.
7. Remember that some boys do not like public praise, and a private word is more appreciated. If this is the case, the school is probably in the grip of anti-swotism (see Chapter 4), in which case there is a considerable amount of work to be done.
8. Try setting homework which actually favours boys and stretches girls, e.g. observe the reaction in class when an essay, notes or all the answers to the comprehension must not total more than ten lines. Boys go home smiling; some of the girls will be beside themselves.

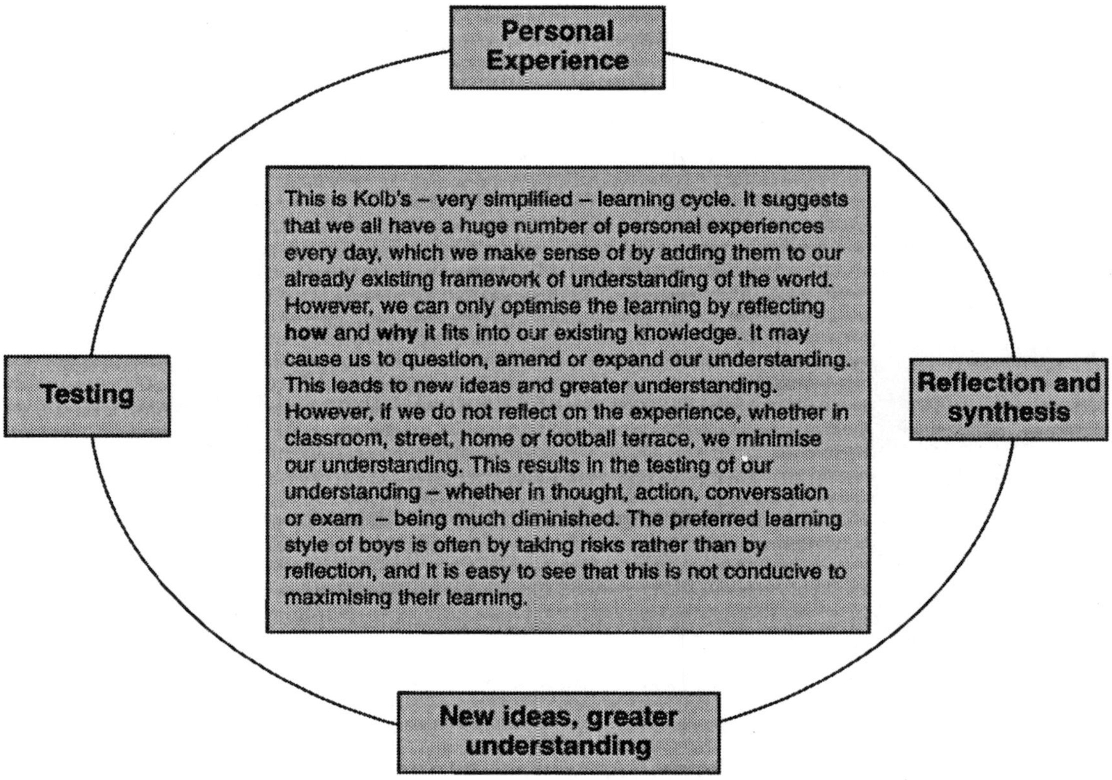
Personal Experience
This is Kolb's – very simplified – learning cycle. It suggests that we all have a huge number of personal experiences every day, which we make sense of by adding them to our already existing framework of understanding of the world. However, we can only optimise the learning by reflecting **how** and **why** it fits into our existing knowledge. It may cause us to question, amend or expand our understanding. This leads to new ideas and greater understanding. However, if we do not reflect on the experience, whether in classroom, street, home or football terrace, we minimise our understanding. This results in the testing of our understanding – whether in thought, action, conversation or exam – being much diminished. The preferred learning style of boys is often by taking risks rather than by reflection, and it is easy to see that this is not conducive to maximising their learning.
Reflection and synthesis
New ideas, greater understanding
Testing

Figure 6.6 Kolb's Learning Cycle

Reflection

Some authors (Hannon 1997, Shaw and Hawes 1998) have pointed out that many boys find it more difficult to reflect than girls do. This is a critical finding, for reflection is one of the most important constituent parts of learning (see Kolb's Learning Cycle, Figure 6.6). If any learner does not have time or capacity to reflect there is a danger that he or she will not optimise the learning from his or her experiences. It is incumbent on teachers to encourage boys to reflect more than many of them would naturally choose to do. This can be achieved in a number of ways, the most important of which is 'hands up in class'.

1. Hands up in class

Hands up can be an excellent way of getting a lesson off to a brisk and even exciting start. In the right classrooms, with good banter, it can lead to humour, relationship building and the cementing of knowledge. We do not suggest that it should be banished, but merely relegated to become *part* of a teacher's menu rather than the mainstay – which it often is – of assessing whole-class understanding.

The problem is that boys love it. It appeals to their preferred risk-taking learning style: unfortunately, they often don't learn very much from it.

Geoff Hannon points out that boys putting their hands up in class is disadvantageous to both genders. The boys are encouraged to speculate but not to reflect, and therefore do not. The girls, whose preferred style is to reflect, do not have that strength recognised nor are they really encouraged to speculate because it is often too risky for them. If the teacher starts the lesson by asking 'What did we learn in the last lesson: no, don't put your hands up now. Turn to your partner(s) and discuss it for 30 seconds. Then put your hand up' – if she or he says that, four things happen which would otherwise not have done:

(a) boys reflect in their discussion;
(b) girls reflect and discuss, and are then more confident to put their hands up because they know that at least one other person agrees with them;
(c) the *whole* class are considering what they learned, probably in a meaningful way, which helps embed the learning;
(d) the correct answer is far more likely to be forthcoming.

2. Paired marking

Another way of getting boys to reflect is by a paired marking scheme, which has the additional benefit of reducing the teacher's marking load. The idea is that each pupil is paired up, after which it follows the same organisational pattern as an American tennis tournament. They have to check each other's work before swapping it with another pair who then mark it against a supplied marking scheme. Pairs score points by correctly finding mistakes and pointing them out to the other pair. Any dispute has to go to the teacher. In the next piece of work, the pairs change partners so that before long, everybody in the class has checked the work of, and had their work checked by, everybody else. The scores a pair get are marked to each individual. In this way boys, and girls, get used to the idea of checking work before it is handed in, and at the same time thinking about work from the perspective of a marker or examiner. It is also good fun and social, getting pupils mixing and working with others in a way they would not usually choose to do.

APPENDIX 6.1

Alphabet semaphore

Write the following sequence of letters on the board and ask pupils to stand up so that they can see it. As you say the alphabet aloud, they have to lift and lower their right, left or both arms – depending on whether it says L, R or B underneath the letter. Go slowly the first time round to make sure they can all keep up and understand what they are doing. Then speed up the second time. Variations on this theme could involve legs, star jumps and hands over eyes.

A	B	C	D	E
L	L	R	B	R
F	G	H	I	J
B	L	R	R	B
K	L	M	N	O
B	B	L	R	L
P	Q	R	S	T
R	L	B	L	R
U	V	W	X	Y
B	L	L	R	R
		Z		
		B		

APPENDIX 6.2

Examples of action points to move towards target grades

Punctuality

- I will get to school by 8.25 a.m. each day.
- I will arrive promptly at each lesson so I am ready to start work.
- I will get up by 7 a.m. so that I am not so rushed in getting to school.

Attendance

- I will make every effort to attend school each day.
- I am aiming for full attendance over the next month.

Organisational skills

- I will make sure that I have checked and packed my bag the night before school, so I have homework to hand in and books for the day.
- I will get all the equipment out promptly at the start of each lesson.
- When I have completed a piece of homework in a subject, I will spend 10 minutes checking and sorting my notes and making a note of any gaps I need to fill.

Listening in class

- I will make sure that I listen intently to what is said in...............................
- After the teacher has spoken I will check that I understand what is being said.

Responding in class

- I will ask and answer in class at least three times a day.
- In...............................I will use questions to check my understanding.

Work partner in class

- If I am being distracted in class I will ask the teacher if I can move.
- I will continue to work well with.........................in ....
- I will not sit with................................or...............................

Seating position in class

- In...........................I will ask to sit nearer to the teacher.
- I will sit well away from...........................and...............................

For the most able

- I will extend my work in..........................by thinking about.....................
- An interesting part of my work in.............................. is ....and I will now find out more about it.
- An academic skill I will develop in the next few weeks is..........................
- A personal/social skill I will develop in the next few weeks is.....................

Use of the student planner

- I will enter all set homework into my planner.
- I will record all deadlines for coursework into my planner.
- As I sit down to start my homework I will check what is to be done that night and which section of longer assignments I need to work on.

Drafting/preparing work

- I will spend the first ten minutes of each homework checking what I have to do and setting time allocations for each piece of work.
- In.................................I will spend ten minutes planning the shape of my work before I start to write it.
- In.................................I will plan the paragraphs of content before I start to write it up.
- I will try brainstorming lists of ideas and then grouping them together before I start to write up work.
- I will use spider diagrams to link ideas together.

Adding more detail to work

- In.................................I will give an example to illustrate each major point I make.
- In.................................I will comment on why the example I have given is a useful one.
- I will find one extra book to consult for my work in...............................

Homework: time spent on it

- I will spend...............................hours on homework on four nights per week. I will also do...............................hours at the end.
- In...............................I will spend an extra half hour on work every Wednesday.
- For the next two weeks I will log the time spent on homework and speak to my teacher/tutor about it.

Homework: use of resources

- For each piece of homework in..............................I will consult two sources before I start to plan my answer.
- I will use the school/town library once a fortnight to help to get resources to support work in...............................
- I will ask my teacher for extra resources to help with homework in..............................

Homework: organisational skills

- I will make my best effort to work in a place without distraction.
- On longer assignments I will break them up into at least four separate tasks and enter them in my Planner as such.
- For longer assignments in..............................I will spend two sessions planning and two sessions writing up.

Revision strategies

- I will revise..............................for 40 minutes, break for 20 minutes, and then spend 10 minutes testing myself on my learning.
- I will speak answers to past questions onto cassette tapes, then check for gaps using my notes.
- I will spend one session per week looking at exam terms such as 'explain', 'comment upon', 'factorise', 'evaluate'.
- I will keep my revision stimulating by making such notes as 'Ten key words from this topic are' or 'the six things I will remember about this topic forever are . . .'.

Revision: organisational skills

- I will draw up a revision timetable seven weeks before my exams and show it to my tutor.
- I will have a copy of my revision timetable in my Planner and one at home.

Outside activities: employment, leisure, commitments

- I will have one evening each week and one full day at weekends away from schoolwork.
- I will cut my job down to.........hours per week until my exams are over.
- I will limit outside commitments to two per week until my exams are over.

Presentational skills: spelling, handwriting, paragraphing

- I will cross out planning notes and mistakes with one neat line.
- In..............................I will make it a priority to write in paragraphs.
- In..............................I will cut down the length of answers I give to questions worth only 1 or 2 marks.

Getting help with work

- I will talk to...............................each Thursday about the successes I have had in.............................during the week.
- I will talk to teachers as soon as possible if I am having problems with homework assignments.

Keeping motivated

- Every Sunday I will quickly write down the main areas of learning which have gone well this week.
- Every fortnight I will tell my teacher/tutor about three things which are going well with my learning and one area which needs further improvement.
- I will talk to people at home, and my friends, about my targets and will share strategies with them.

Conclusion

This book has taken the reader on a brief excursion through the complicated topography of boys' under-achievement. We hope that it has been more than a fleeting visit and that we have presented some practical and coherent strategies that can make a difference in schools.

We hope that the main learning points are:

1. A recognition of the importance of data and the uses to which it can be put.
2. That the origins of boys' under-achievement are complex and will not be fixed by short-term strategies.
3. That raising boys' achievement is a window to good practice.
4. That raising boys' achievement will also help to raise that of girls.
5. That careful planning is as important as the action taken.
6. That raising boys' achievement is a perfectly practical, ordinary example of project management.
7. That the process of raising boys' achievement offers teachers the chance to rediscover themselves as reflective practitioners.

Boys are only one discernible group that under-achieves and work has to be done for *all* such pupils. We hope that this book may be a contribution to raising their achievement as well. Above all we hope that the book has been both accessible and has made a contribution to raising achievement in school.

Bibliography

Arnot, M. *et al.* (1998) *Recent Research on Gender and Educational Performance.* London: OFSTED.

Barton, P. and Coley, R. (1992) via http://ericweb.tc.columbia.edu/families/strong/key_research.html

Basic Skills Agency (2000) *Quality Mark for Primary Schools. Case study guides. Element nine: involving parents.* London: BSA.

Bastiani, J. (1983) 'Listening to parents: philosophy, critique and method'. PhD thesis, University of Nottingham.

Biddulph, S. (1997) *Raising Boys.* London: Thorsons.

Blair, M. and Bourne, J. (1998) *Making the Difference: teaching and learning strategies in successful multi-ethnic schools.* London: Open University/DfEE.

Bleach, K. *et al.* (1996) *What Difference Does it Make? An investigation of factors influencing the motivation and performance of Year 8 boys in a West Midlands comprehensive school.* University of Wolverhampton Educational Research Unit.

Bleach, K. *et al.* (1998) *Raising Boys' Achievement in Schools.* Stoke-on-Trent: Trentham Books.

Boaler, J. (1996) *Setting, Social, Class and Survival of the Quickest.* London: King's College.

Bradford, W. A. (1995) 'The progress of boys in secondary school'. Dissertation for MEd, University of Huddersfield.

Bradford, W. A. (1996) *Raising Boys' Achievement.* Kirklees Local Education Authority.

Bush, T. and West-Burnham, J. (1994) *The Principles of Educational Management.* Harlow: Longman.

DfEE (1999) *National Healthy School Standard: guidance.* London: DfEE.

DfEE (2000a) *Autumn Package of Pupil Performance Information.* London: DfEE.

DfEE (2000b) *Statistics of Education. Public examinations GCSE/GNVQ and GCE/AGNVQ in England 1999.* London: The Stationery Office.

DfEE (2001) *Parental Involvement* http://www.standards.dfee.gov.uk/parentalinvolvement/pwp/pwp_home.html

EOC *Research Findings. Gender and Differential Achievement in Education and Training: a research review,* ISBN 1 870358 80 5.

EOC in Wales (1999) *Different but Equal,* ISBN 1 870358 97 X.

EOC/OFSTED (1996*) The Gender Divide. Performance differences between girls and boys at school.* London: HMSO.

Epstein, D. *et al.* (eds) (1998) *Failing Boys? Issues in gender and achievement.* Buckingham: Open University Press.

Frater, G. (1997) *Improving Boys' literacy.* London: Basic Skills Agency.

Frater, G. (2000) *Securing Boys' Literacy.* London: Basic Skills Agency.

Gillborn, D. and Mirza, H. S. (2000) *Educational Inequality: mapping race, class and gender.* London: Institute of Education, University of London.

Haigh, G. (1975) *The School and the Parent.* Oxford: Pitman.

Hannon, G. (1997) *The Gender Game and How to Win It.* (Published by author)

Kirklees LEA (1996) *Guidelines for Schools: Involving parents in children's education.* Kirklees LEA.

Kirklees LEA (March/April 2001) *Kirklees Parent.* Kirklees LEA.

Klein, R. (1995) 'Tales of snips and snails', *Times Educational Supplement,* 9 June, English Supplement, p. 4.

Klein, R. (2000a) 'Lost at school', in *Education Futures: lifelong learning.* London: RSA/Design Council.

Klein, R. (2000b) *Defying Disaffection: how schools are winning the hearts and minds of reluctant students.* Stoke-on-Trent: Trentham Books.

Kress, G. (1998) 'The future still belongs to boys', *The Independent,* 11 June, 4–5.

McCourt, F. (1997) *Angela's Ashes.* London: Flamingo.

McGeaney, P. (1969) *Parents Are Welcome.* London and Harlow: Green & Co, Longmans.

Millard, E. (1997) *Differently Literate: boys, girls and the schooling of literacy.* London: Falmer Press.

Noble, C. (1998) 'Raising boys' achievement in the primary school', in Bleach, K. (ed.) *Raising Boys' Achievement in School,* Stoke-on-Trent: Trentham Books.

Noble, C. (2001) Unpublished notes of ministerial seminar on boys' achievement, 6 February 2001.

Noble, C. and Bradford, W. (2000) *Getting It Right for Boys . . . and Girls.* London: Routledge.

Noble, C. and Massett, K. (2001) *Encouraging Pupil Responsibility*. Oxford: Heinemann.

The Observer (25 February 2001) 'Better-off families breed Britain's new hooligans', p. 7.

OFSTED (2001) *Statistical Profile for Education in Schools*. London: OFSTED.

Pickering, J. and Lodge, C. (1998) *Improving Schools*, vol. 1, no. 1. London: Institute of Education. University of London.

Shaw, S. and Hawes, T. (1998) *Teaching and Learning in the Primary Classroom*. Optimal Learning.

Tice, L. (1997) *Investment in Excellence*. Seattle: The Pacific Institute.

Topping, K. (1988) *The Peer Tutoring Handbook*. London: Routledge.

Yates, A. and Pidgeon, D. A. *Transfer at Eleven Plus: a summary of evidence provided by research. Educational Research*, NFER VI, 1958.

Index

Printed in the United Kingdom
by Lightning Source UK Ltd.
111749UKS00001B/3-10